ST ALBION
PARISH NEWS

Book Two

PREFACE BY THE VICAR

WHO would have thought that my first book of collected Parish Newsletters would be so successful?

Not me certainly! Obviously, I hoped it would do well (and I thought it was pretty good!), but never in my wildest dreams did I imagine that it would be the parish's number one bestseller and be described by one reviewer (a Mr A. Campbell in the Newsletter itself) as "without doubt the best book I have ever written". I think he meant "read", don't you?

And as I went around the parish, meeting the good folk who constitute my flock, more and more of you said "Vicar, I hope there's going to be a sequel this Christmas."

Well, here it is!

Let me quote what one impartial critic (Mr Mandelson) said when I showed him the manuscript: "I have never read anything as uplifting as this brilliant collection. Can I have my job back?"

Enjoy!

Tony

Published in Great Britain by
Private Eye Productions Ltd, 6 Carlisle Street, W1V 5RG.
© 1999 Pressdram Ltd
ISBN 1 901784 15 0
Designed by Bridget Tisdall
Printed in England by Ebenezer Baylis & Son Ltd, Worcester
2 4 6 8 10 9 7 5 3 1

ST ALBION PARISH NEWS

Book Two

Further letters from the vicar,
the Rev. A.R.P. Blair MA (Oxon)

compiled for

PRIVATE EYE

by Ian Hislop, Richard Ingrams,
Christopher Booker and Barry Fantoni

PLANS FOR
THE NEW NOTICEBOARD
IN THE VESTRY

Designed by the vicar and made possible by a kind donation from an anonymous well-wisher *(G. Robinson).*

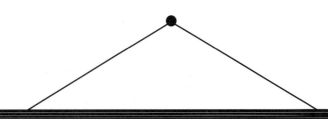

NAMES OF PREVIOUS INCUMBENTS

CANON HAROLD MACMILLAN	1957-63
REV. ALEC DOUGLAS-HOME	1963-4
REV. J. H. WILSON	1964-70
REV. GROCER HEATH	1970-4
REV. J. H. WILSON (AGAIN)	1974-6
REV. JAMES CALLAGHAN	1976-9
DEACONESS MARGARET HILDA THATCHER	1979-90
REV. JOHN MAJOR	1990-7

REV. A.R.P. BLAIR
M.A. OXON   1997-

ST ALBION PARISH NEWS

18th September 1998

Hullo!

Well, isn't it tremendous that the football season is with us again!

From the park come the shouts of young boys — and girls! — enjoying one of God's greatest games.

"Man on!", "Chop him!", "Bring him down!" Don't all of us thrill to hear these young people learning the basic principles of teamwork, fair play and selflessness!

Look, that's what football is all about — particularly here at St Albion's, — which is why we are all so keen on the game. I don't go on about football in my sermons because I'm trying to be popular! Heavens no! I've loved football since I saw Sheffield Tuesday play Manchester Rovers when I was a boy!

All of which brings me on to my second theme this week, which is my own popularity in the parish.

I am told that one of our house focus groups, under Mrs Dee Moss, has reported that I am no longer "top of the pops", and that in the last few weeks my popularity rating is no higher than that of my predecessor, the Rev. Major.

Let me tell you this. You don't get anywhere in this life by listening to focus groups and trying to be popular!

Let's not forget that Our Lord himself would have not scored very highly on any popularity poll!

I think you'll recall that a certain Mr Barabbas won the approval of the multitude when they called for a show of hands!

The important thing surely is to do what you believe in, not what you think will please people!

That way you will be far more popular in the end, which is what really counts!

Why don't we all think about that every night before we go to bed, and then write to Mrs Moss telling her what we think about her silly focus group!

Your friend,

Tony

Nothing gets past Tony!

You Write...

From Mr Benn,

Dear Sir,
I would like to protest at the way we were all called back from our holidays for the Extraordinary General Meeting of the PCC, only so that we could rubber stamp a series of decisions about important church business already made by the Vicar on his own. There was a time when
Yours faithfully,
T. Benn, Scargill Villas.
■ The editor Mr Campbell reserves the right to cut any letters for reasons of space.

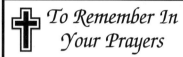 *To Remember In Your Prayers*

Mr Cook, who, rather than attend the important oecumenical conference in Austria, chose instead to go on holiday with his new wife. Let us hope Robin had a good rest, and that he will eventually come to see how self-indulgent and irresponsible it was of him to put swanning about like a lovesick teenager above his parish duties. T.B.

Our Thanks...

...to **Mr Jenkins** for all the work he has put into his paper on new voting procedures for the PCC and other parish elections. Copies of his 398 page report are available from the Vestry (price £25). But for those who have not got time to read all his excellent recommendations in detail, he has provided a helpful summary personally dictated by Roy to Mr Campbell from his room in the St Albion's Sunset Home For Retired Gentlefolk:

● What I would wecommend most stwongly is that we intwoduce a system of single transfewwable voting (or AMG). Under this, each elector has one vote, which can be twansferred whensoever it may be appwopwiate and added to the votes cast for the vicar or his fwiends, until such time as he secures an overwhelming pwoportion of the total vote. W.J

Thank you, Roy, and a case of your favourite "claret" is winging its way to you to show our appreciation for all your good work. T.B.

MILLENNIUM TENT NEWS

Mr Murdoch, the owner of the Adult Mags and Vids Centre, has kindly agreed to supply the material for the "Adult Zone" which will celebrate the human body by means of videos. Thanks Rupert! T. B.

PARISH OUTING — CHANGE OF VENUE

Please note that, at the insistence of Mr Prescott, this year's outing will be to Blackpool not Florence after all. I know some of us will be less than thrilled at the thought of all those smelly fish and chips and dirty old trams. But, as John rightly says, it is important to show that we are in touch with ordinary folk! T.B.

PS. Would any businessmen like to sponsor the outing? You will get to sit next to Tony at the very front of the bus!

P.M.

THE MILLENNIUM TENT APPEAL

Local artist Brian Bagnall shows us how it's going!

Well on the way to the target! T.B.

ST ALBION PARISH NEWS

2nd October 1998

Hullo!

As I am sure you all know, I have just come back from America, where I played a leading part in what could turn out to be the most important top-level oecumenical conference ever held!

The subject was our old friend the "Third Way". Or perhaps I should say "our new friend" because the vision of the Third Way is about as new as you can get!

It was a fantastic experience! There was I, the vicar of St Albion's in England, having the chance to tell some of the most important religious leaders in the world all about an idea which began right here, back home, in our own vicarage!

Who says a prophet isn't recognised in other people's countries? I certainly was! Everyone there agreed that my "Third Way" was just about the most exciting, visionary, world-changing idea they had ever heard!

No one was keener on the idea than my American "buddy" the Reverend William Jefferson Clinton of the Church of the Seven Day Fornicators.

He told us what a relief it was to talk about something that was really meaningful, after all the trouble he has been having with his congregation trying to get him de-frocked for having an inappropriate relationship with a female member of his Church's Family Values Youth Group! We all gave him a big hand, which he said was always something he appreciated!

So I've come back all fired up to take the "Third Way" message into the Third Millennium!

Here in St Albion's we are going to launch a campaign to spread the Third Way round a new spiritual training course which, even though it is voluntary, I expect every member of the parish to attend.

Some of you may have come across the "Alpha Course". Well, our version is even better, which is why we've called it the "Albion Course".

I don't want to say too much about this, because it might sound too much like blowing one's own trumpet! So, I've asked our Editor Mr Campbell to set out the basics in a rather clever format below my newsletter.

See you on the course! *Tony*

(And I don't mean the one where you play golf!)

WHAT IS ALBION?

Anyone interested in finding out more about The "Third Way".

Learning and laughter. It's possible to learn about Tony's ideas and have fun at the same time. But you mustn't laugh at the "Third Way" — that is neither clever nor helpful.

Blair. The name of our vicar and the inventor of the "Third Way".

Indispensable, which is what the Third Way is! And also idiots, which is what everyone who attacks the Third Way are (see our prayer for Mr Mortimer!).

Olives with Organic Bread! Finger food for those happy evenings when parishioners will get together in small groups to find out more about the Third Way, the Truth and the Life!

No one is to be left out, except those who are so lazy as not to turn up, or so silly as that they know better than the Vicar. (See prayers for Mr Mortimer.)

**Who was it who said,
"I am Albion and Omega,
the beginning and
the end?"**

(For answer see Vicar's Website
www.swingingtony@stalbion.co.uk)

B.B

NOTICES

■ Our Harvest Festival will be on October 5 at 11am. The Vicar wishes it to be known that genetically modified produce is perfectly acceptable so long as it is clearly labelled as such (let's not live in the past, farmers and allotment holders!). Also, anyone wishing to bring *no* produce is free to do so, in thanksgiving for the blessing of set-aside.

The Vicar has written a special chorus which we shall sing after the presentation of the cheque to Church funds from the Area Representative of Monsanto:

"We plough the fields and scatter
The improved seed on the land.
So let's not be unreasonable
And try to get it banned."

CHURCH OUTING TO BLACKPOOL

By the time you read this, the church outing will have been a great success! Everyone will have had a marvellous time and there will have been no trouble on the bus! There will be a full report in our next issue.

Meantime, thank you to the sponsors, especially Mr Somerfield, who generously paid for the plastic name badges and the smart baseball caps issued to all parishioners. These, by the way, have replaced the old-fashioned Kiss-Me-Quick hats so popular with Mr Prescott and his fellow members of the Working Men's Club.

To Remember In Your Prayers

Mr Mortimer, who has been "having doubts" and, foolishly, expressing them in local newspapers. Let's hope he soon regains his trust in Tony and realises that it is the duty of every parishioner to keep very quiet when their faith deserts them.

ST ALBION PARISH NEWS

16th October 1998

Hullo!

Well, I'm back again after another very important mission, carrying the message of the "Third Way" to our brethren in distant China!

And it is distant, believe me! Seventeen hours in an aeroplane gave Cherie and me plenty of time to think about the great and ancient civilisation we were about to visit, and what we could do to improve their lot!

And there are a lot of them, mark my words!

200 billion of them, if I got my figures right!

I know some of you are deeply concerned about China's alleged record on human rights, and the way the authorities are supposed to persecute those who share our beliefs.

Let me say at once that I share your concern, and I was determined to raise the matter with our hosts when a suitable opportunity arose.

But, look, if you're invited to a party, you don't immediately start criticising your hosts' choice of dips, or the quality of the drinks they are serving!

One thing I've learned, travelling around the world, is that different people have different ways of doing things. "Judge not, that ye be not judged." Whoever said that certainly had a good point!

Anyway, Cherie and I really enjoyed ourselves! We were lucky enough to visit the Great Wall, which is a truly remarkable sight. How many of us, I couldn't help wondering, have a "great wall" in our own lives, dividing us from our fellows. I thought it might make a good chorus for our next family service!

> "There is a Great Wall far away
> That all of us must climb.
> A great Wall far away
> A wall as old as time.

CHORUS

> *Climb, climb, climb the wall*
> *Climb it every day.*
> *Climb, climb, climb the wall*
> *At work and rest and play!"*

But I'm sorry to have to say that when Cherie and I touched base back at the Vicarage, we found a pretty negative atmosphere in the parish.

A lot of you have got it into your heads that the parish finances are not in quite such good shape as Mr Brown has been telling us all.

There are doubts as to whether we will be able to afford some of the projects we have budgeted for, like spending more money on the primary school and the cottage hospital.

Well, all I can say is that, if Mr Brown has got his sums wrong, then it's no fault of mine!

I can't be everywhere at once in the parish, but I can assure you that I will be keeping a very close check on our treasurer in the coming weeks and if changes have to be made, I will not hesitate to think very carefully about making them!

So let us remember that when I took over the parish a year ago, things were in a pretty bad way, and it's bound to take a little time to sort it all out!

Don't forget the words of Our Lord, "You have nothing to fear but fear itself" *(New Deal Bible)*.

      Yours,

        Tony

Greetings From Peking

SWEET AND SOUR
Guess who's the sweet one?

From The Churchwarden

It has been brought to my attention that people are complaining about an alleged misuse of parish raffle funds. Just because we made it clear that this money would only go to local charities, they are now complaining that we are using it to pay off general parish expenses. I would like to make it clear that there is nothing wrong with this, and if the Vicar and I decide to spend the money in this way, then that's our affair and no one else's.

So in future I would be grateful if parishioners would mind their own business.

P Mandelson, Churchwarden

✝ To Remember In Your Prayers

Mrs Short, who in a moment of thoughtlessness and lack of compassion made an unprovoked attack on the Vicar's dear and close friend Rev William Jefferson Clintstone III of the Church of Seven Day Fornicators. Clare has since written to Tony apologising. Let us all remember the words of the Good Book, "People who live in glass houses shouldn't cast the first stone" *(Proverbs)*. After all, Clare wouldn't like us to raise issues of her own private life (eg, her love child), would she? T.B.

PARISH OUTING TO BLACKPOOL DIARY

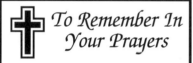

by Mr Prescott of the Working Men's Club

We arrived seven hours late, no thanks to Mr So-Called Branson and his trains. In future, I for one will be travelling by car, thank you very much! Still, spirits were high as we all caught our first glimpse of the famous "tower".

We were all looking forward to a bit of a knees-up and a few pints. But, no offence to the Vicar, when he got up and gave his little talk that was meant to cheer us all up, it frankly all fell a bit flat. Fortunately, yours truly was on hand to save the day with a few jokes (some of them at Tony's expense!) and everyone went home feeling they had had quite a good time after all. J.P.

You Write...

From Mr T. Banks

Dear Sir,

Call me old-fashioned if you like, but I never thought I would live to see the day when, on our parish outing, I was expected to wear a name tag sponsored by a local supermarket. Whose crazy idea was

Yours sincerely
Tony Banks Chair,
St Albion's Playing
Field Committee

■ The editor Mr Campbell reserves the right to cut any letters for reasons of space.

ST ALBION PARISH NEWS

30th October 1998

Hullo!

Well, we all turned our clocks back on Sunday so the nights are drawing in, the leaves are falling from the trees, and it's hard not to feel a little bit gloomy!

I'm sure that's why a number of people around the parish are saying "Vicar (*Tony*, please!), am I right in saying that hard times are coming?"

And I say to them, "Yes, of course they're not!" And I'll tell you why! It's only natural that nights get darker, leaves fall off the trees and people lose their jobs!

As the book of Excusiastes says, "There is a time and a place for everything." (7.14)

"A time to laugh and a time to cry; a time to dance and a time to get the sack".

Do you remember it was a song by the Seekers? I used to play it on my guitar at our Student Fellowship Cheese and Wine Evenings to welcome the freshmen and the overseas students! (And I played it rather well actually!)

So, look, there are obviously going to be a few rough patches in our lives, particularly our financial lives, when things don't go quite as well as Mr Brown told us all they would!

You can't blame the vicar for that! It would be like blaming me for the weather!

And, remember, what comes after winter? It's springtime, of course, when the sun comes out, the birds begin to sing and everyone gets their jobs back!

So, it'll all turn out fine in the end! Trust me, folks!

Or, if you don't trust me, trust the Good Book, where it says, "All's well that ends well"!

And let's think again about this business of putting the clocks back.

Surely, in a real sense, we shouldn't be putting the clock of our Life *back*. No, that's just like wanting to go back to the bad old days, when people expected the vicar to look after them, and run their lives for them!

(Some of our old folk still hanker after those days! Mr Benn and Mrs Castle may know who I'm thinking of!)

But what we need, in the spirit of the new St Albion's, is to put the clock *forward*, to the next millennium and beyond!

That's what I've tried to get across in a special chorus I've written for this Sunday's evensong (which will begin symbolically at 4 o'clock, instead of 6.30!).

> "Forward, forward go the clocks
> Upward we must pull our socks!
> Skies may be black, but never fear,
> Springtime days will soon be here!
> ©Words and Music Rev. A.R.P. Blair 1998

See you Sunday!
Yours,

Tony

 # Millennium Tent

■ My thanks to the **Hinduja brothers** who run the Cash 'n' Carry in the trading estate for their very generous donation to the religious stall in our Millennium Tent. They won't be forgotten. If they ever want a place in the Sunset Home, I am sure the Vicar will be happy to arrange it!

■ Thanks also to **Mr Ronald McDonald**, the local manager of the Burger Bar in the High Street who has very generously agreed to provide refreshment in the Millennium Tent. Mr McDonald wishes nothing in return for his support other than the whole event be renamed *"The Happy Meal Tent Experience"*. The PCC saw no problems with this admirable suggestion.

Mr Mandelson, Churchwarden

Writes TB: *"After all didn't Our Lord feed the five thousand with a simple Fish 'n' Bap takeaway meal — soft drink not included? I think he did. Let's stop moaning about this and simply "HAVE A NICE DAY!"*

You Write...

Dear Vicar,

Some of us have recently got together to produce a little pamphlet, to restate the core doctrines which once used to inspire our Church. We feel the central tenets of our traditional creed have been jettisoned to make way for a wishy-washy

Yours faithfully,
E. Hobsbawm,
pp "Marxism In St Albion Today",
The Old Gulag.

■ The Editor reserves the right to cut any letters on the grounds of length. A.C.

THE VICAR ADDS: "It is sad to think that there are still people who believe in an old man with a beard sitting in the British Museum, and telling us all how to live our lives!"
T.B.

✠ To Remember In Your Prayers

Mr Meale who has got into trouble trying to help out his friends from the Greek Tavern "Freebios". Let us hope he comes to realise that you cannot mix friendship with church business (unless you are the vicar obviously which is entirely different!)

Old Folks Update!

*T*he Vicar is very sorry to hear about the lack of co-operation being shown by some of the residents of our *Sunset Home for Distressed Gentlefolk*, just because we are asking them to vacate the building. Some of them have been scribbling on the walls, making a noise at night and even being personally offensive to the new matron Mrs Jay.

One or two of them have even suggested that Mrs Jay has no real qualifications for her job. This is completely untrue. Mrs Jay is a very old friend of Tony's, and what better qualification could anyone have than that? Other people are asking who is going to be put into the home, when some of the more tiresome current residents are evicted.

The answer is that a fairer system will be worked out in due course, whereby the Vicar himself will decide each case on merit. As Mrs Jay (old Rev. Callaghan's daughter!) puts it "this is better than getting in just because of who your father was".

Mr Cunningham,
Parish Enforcer

Notices

■ *There will be a service of reconciliation at St. Albion's conducted jointly by the Vicar and the leading Argentinian Minister Father Menem. In order to promote a real feeling of harmony and togetherness there will be no mention at all in the service of the unfortunate Islands that gave rise to so much unpleasantness in the past.* TB

Parish Scrapbook

More tea, vicar?
Tony shows his support for the Reverend William Jefferson Clinton of the Church of The Seven Day Fornicators. Says Tony, "Bill tells me that he truly repents of his sins and denies that he has committed any sins in the first place. He also tells me that he is very keen to try the Third Way, as he has never done it like that before!"

Keep it up, Cherie! (we're all football crazy)

"Sikh and Ye Shall Find" *(Book of The Dome, 7.11).* I hope it works for donations to the tent!

ST ALBION PARISH NEWS

13th November 1998

Hullo!

I can only have one theme this week, and that is the importance of the family!

As you may know, I have chosen this week as "The Week of the Family", as a time for us all to think about what the family means nowadays.

So, let's begin with what it DOESN'T mean!

Some people still have a cosy picture in their minds of a smiling group sitting round the kitchen table, with mum making cakes and dad home from the office smoking his pipe, and watching the children as they sit doing their homework or making model aeroplanes out of balsa wood!

And of course there's a lot to be said for that old-fashioned type of family! A stable home and two loving parents married to each other is the best possible start in life for a child!

But it's not the only one! For instance, there are plenty of people these days who are bringing up kids in very different ways!

They may have chosen not to get married.

Or they may have fallen out of love with each other, and chosen to live with someone else's husband or wife or partner (like Mr Cook and Mr Lairg!).

Or, again, they may have a partner of the same sex (like Mr Smith, although he doesn't have any children yet!).

Or they may have no partner at all, and be successfully bringing up children on their own.

The last thing I want to do is to tell people how they should live their lives.

Look! Of course marriage is the best option. But then so are all the other options!

It's not my job to preach — but I know that many people look to me for guidance and advice on how to live their lives!

That's why I have set up a new team of counsellors, to help everyone in the parish to think through their own personal situations vis à vis relationships, partners, kids and the importance of getting married (should that be their preferred option!).

After all, didn't Our Lord himself attend a wedding at Cana (and enhance the catering facilities!), which shows that he can't have thought marriage was all bad!

But also he was unmarried himself, and his mother was a single mum, even though she was married to her partner (Joseph), who, of course, was present at the birth!

So what is my message on this vital issue of the family? What I am saying is that there is no room for any fudge or compromise!

We have to make it quite clear that we are going to support the family, in whatever shape or form it appears!

As the Good Book says, "It takes all sorts to make a world". *(Book of Revelations, Ch. 12).*

So, let's go out and preach the message, that we're all one Big Happy Family!

Yours,

Tony

(happily married father of 3, who nevertheless refuses to be judgemental about others less fortunate!)

FROM THE CHURCHWARDEN MR MANDELSON
PARISH OUTINGS

There will be no more outings of anyone in the parish by anyone. I hope this is understood. It has been brought to my notice that some people in the parish are spreading malicious and unhelpful rumours about my own private life. I wish to make it clear that I do not wish to say anything more about this matter, and I do not expect anyone else to either. You have been warned. P.M.

Congratulations!

Well done to **Mr Brown** (Nick *not* Gordon obviously!) for coming out and telling us that he has come out! It is none of our business, but even so it takes a lot of courage and a threat from a local newspaper to admit in public what you get up to in private. Well done, Nick! You are the third member of the PCC this week! What one might call "The Third Gay"! Let this be an example to everyone else. T.B.

A Message From Mrs Jay, Matron of the St Albion's Sunset Home For Distressed Gentlefolk

My thanks to everyone who has supported my plans for the reorganisation of our retirement home. I know one or two people have complained about the proposed changes, particularly some of the old folk who are being asked to move out. I certainly agree that not all of them are as hopeless and stupid as they have been painted, but most of them are and they are only getting their just desserts.

I am also extremely annoyed at the way people are still suggesting that I was only given the job of running the Sunset Home because my father was once the vicar and I am therefore in a position of privilege. My appointment was nothing to do with this, and anyone who says it is is as stupid and hopeless as all those people I am quite rightly asking to vacate to make way for more deserving cases like myself.

M. Jay (Daughter of Rev. Callaghan)

✝ To Remember In Your Prayers

Mr Davies, formerly of our PCC, who has let the parish down very badly after an incident in the waste ground behind the church, the details of which are too unpleasant to be included in a family newsletter such as this! Of course, what Mr Davies chooses to do in his private life is entirely his own affair. It has nothing whatever to do with his duties as a member of the PCC, but I know you will all understand that I had no alternative but to sack him. Mr Davies came to me for confession but he did not tell me the full story. Or if he did I must have forgotten it. Either way it was an outrageous breach of trust and Mr. Campbell (who sometimes sits next to me on these occasions) was quite right to tell Ron to resign at once for whatever it is that he has done.

T.B.

PCC Elections

Mr Rhodri Morgan has let it be known that he wishes to be considered for the vacancy left by Mr Davies. I know Rhodi may be popular with some people in the parish, but popularity isn't everything! Our new rules make it clear that the successful candidate, whoever he or she may be, will be the person the churchwarden and I decide is most fitted for this post. I am sorry Rhodri, but rules are rules! T.B.

ST ALBION PARISH NEWS

27th November 1998

Hello!

Well it has been quite a week hasn't it and I don't mind admitting that at the beginning of it, I was feeling a little bit tired. After all, it's a pretty demanding job trying to run this parish, and it's a job that some of you are not making any easier. I'm not naming names, but I think Mr Livingstone, Mr Morgan and a number of residents from the Old People's Home will know who I mean! Anyway it was very kind of various members of the PCC to express their concern that I was being overstretched, and to offer to step in and take over some of my duties. Their kind thoughts made me feel a lot better immediately and I am no longer tired at all.

No, if I am anything, I am angry. And what am I angry about?

Let me tell you what I am <u>NOT</u> angry about. I'm not angry because I am not getting my own way at the parish, as some people have suggested. I'm not angry at having all my plans for the parish rejected by people who don't know what they're talking about. So let's get that clear, before we go any further! No. What makes me angry — and sad — is that all the effort that we are putting in to make St Albion's a more efficient, modern, pivotal parish — and dare I say it, a "sexy" place to be! — All these efforts are being undermined by people complaining that there isn't enough democracy in this church. Look, I'm as much a believer in democracy and in people having the right to choose as the next man. But if we choose lots of people with different views, all arguing the toss, what sort of democracy is that? After all, Our Lord picked 12 disciples to follow him, not to argue with him! And wasn't that a perfect example of what I call a "closed list". We don't find any stories in the Bible about the good people of Palestine being invited to elect the disciples — and if we do find anything in the Bible like that, I think it would be only right that we should cut it out!

Look! The point I'm making is spelled out absolutely clearly in the words of the parable, "Many are called, but only a few selected names are chosen." *(Book of Despots 7.14)*.

So, let me put it all in a nutshell. Of course, I want you all to be involved in the parish. In our focus groups. On our flower rota. Doing all the humdrum jobs that are necessary to keep the parish running smoothly. And of course I want you to choose who does which jobs. All I am asking is that you choose the same people that I do ! It's your parish, I'm just here to run it!

Yours

Tony

The vicar agrees that church finances are looking healthy!

A Message from Mrs. Jay, Matron of the St. Albion's Home for Distressed Gentlefolk

*L*ike the Vicar, I'm not angry with the old people for the way they have behaved in the last few weeks and in particular I am not angry with them for disagreeing with me in public. However I do think it might be for the best if the Vicar closed the place down and threw the troublemakers out onto the streets. *(Straight talking there, Margaret! T.B.)*

P.S. Mr Robinson tells me that the Home is on a prime site, and could be turned into a first-class supermarket.

M.Jay (Daughter of Rev.Callaghan)

NOTICES

■ **Mr Blunkett**, the Chairman of our School Governors, would like to inform parents that in future, any pupils found taking drugs on school premises will be dealt with extremely strictly. Offenders will be instantly given counselling, and repeated offenders will be asked to see P.C. Straw, who understands all about these problems.

■ *Good news* from **Mr Dobson** who runs the St Albion's Hospice. There's been a great improvement on the waiting list front. The waiting list is now only 780 people. This represents a significant decrease from last year's figure of 700. (Well done, Frank! T.B.)

■ *More Good News* from **Mr Brown**, our Treasurer, who tells me that our church finances are in excellent shape, regardless of the fact that we're a bit short of money.

FROM THE CHURCHWARDEN

I am not going to Brazil this week because I have discovered that I have an extremely important session of the PCC Sub-Committee On Hassocks to attend. My decision to cancel my trip has nothing to do with the rumours being spread about me and my Brazilian friend by certain parishioners in the Cool Britannia Arms, I have no particular desire to go to Brazil anyway. I shall not be discussing Brazil in this space again. I hope that is clear. P.M.

 ## To Remember In Your Prayers

Let us remember in our prayers all those who are in hardship or in difficulty, especially our friend Mr Robinson, who has suffered a terrible loss of memory over some of his business dealings. Let us give thanks for his full and frank apology and let us remember that he had done nothing wrong and therefore had nothing to apologise for.

Let us remember also our American friend, the Reverend William Jefferson Clinton of the Church of the Seven Day Fornicators, and help him to put the past behind him so that he can move forward. Help us to remember that, like Mr Robinson, he had done nothing and help us to forgive him for whatever it is he didn't do.

ST ALBION PARISH NEWS

11th December 1998

Hullo!

It's Advent again and, as you know, Advent is the time when we look forward, the time when we in the parish make plans for the year ahead. And, let's be honest, there isn't going to be time to do everything. Remember that passage from the Old Testament, "For every thing there is a season: but not for some things obviously". Those wonderful words from the Book of Elasticus *(7,11)*. As true today as they were when they were written all those millions of years ago!

Lots of you have put in some marvellous suggestions — Mr Prescott's idea for scrapping the church car park and building a cycle lane through the churchyard was terrific. But, apologies to John, that one will have to go on the back burner.

Look! It's all about what we've got time for. It's not about personalities. The fact that John told everyone in the Working Men's Club that my ideas about the Third Way are no good has got nothing to do with it! As I told John, there is the first way of doing things — My Way. The second way of doing things — His Way. And the third way of doing things. Which is the same as the First Way!

Anyway, Christmas will soon be upon us and its message is particularly relevant this year "Peace on Earth, Goodwill to Men". And that means our French friends, our Belgian friends, our Swedish friends and even our German friends!

I've recently been attending oecumenical meetings all over Europe and I tell you, it's pretty exciting to see all the old prejudices and divisions breaking down. And that's what one German pastor, Father Oskar said to me. "Tony," he said, "isn't it wunderbar?" (That means "wonderful" in English, in case any of you were wondering.)

He said, "Tony, we are all one big, happy country, I mean family, now — and don't you forget it!"

I haven't forgotten it and I'd like you all to remember it this Christmas!

Cheers!

Tony

A Sinner Repenteth!

Our hearts were all warmed this week when our Parish solicitor, Mr Lairg, of Lairg, Over and Co., publicly confessed how guilty he felt about running off with the wife of another parishioner, i.e. Mrs Dewar. In a moving apology, he said, "It was just one of those things. And it was all a long time ago. I don't know why everyone keeps going on about it."

Well said, Derry! Better one "sinner" who repenteth than a hundred righteous men who aren't friends of mine! T.B.

A Statement From Our Treasurer, Mr Brown

Certain people are putting it about that my assistant Mr Robinson is shortly to be relieved of his position, owing to various alleged 'irregularities' in his dealings with the Inland Revenue, the PCC, the late Robert Maxwell and his erstwhile Belgian lady friend Madame de Legovaire. I would like to make it clear that I have complete confidence in Geoffrey, whatever the Vicar, the Church-warden and the editor of this newsletter mayxcanabgncomptengo bbledygookmosh

(A.C. writes: We apologise that, owing to the Millennium Bug, a number of items in the current newsletter may make no sense at all. Mr Brown's contribution in particular reads like gibberish. Sorry! Ed.)

St Albion's Primary School Carol Concert

The Chairman of Governors Mr Blunkett writes: "This event was a huge success! I think we're all agreed that the highlight was the Vicar and I singing a duet of the Special St Albion's Carol — *"The First of May!"*

X X X X THANKS X X X X

● Our thanks to all the local businessmen like **Mr Murdoch**, from *Adult Mags and Vids Shop* in the High Street, who have given so generously to the Tent fund, with no thought of reward for themselves. So you won't hear the Vicar calling for Mr Murdoch's premises to be closed down! Also it seems that the owner of the very popular burger bar in the High Street, who wants to remain anonymous, has generously offered to provide all the catering for our millennium celebrations, for free. And all we have to do is to call it the Big Mac-llennium Tent (*No problem! T.B.*)

FROM OUR POSTBAG...

Dear Sir,

I would like to remind you that I am still available to play the part of Lord Mayor in the St Albion's Christmas pantomime. Not only have I played him before, with some considerable success, but I also now have a petition signed by over

> *Yours sincerely,*
> *Ken Livingstone,*
> *The Aquatic Pet Centre,*
> *Newts R Us,*
> *The High Street.*

The Editor reserves the right to cut all letters for reasons of space. A.C.

✝ *To Remember In Your Prayers*

LET US particularly remember this week a very unfortunate young man who has got into trouble with his elders and betters in a way which has left him looking rather foolish.

There is no need for me to embarrass him by mentioning his name, but I think we all know who young William Hague is.

LET US remember those who have been given responsibilities that are far too much for them, and who may well shortly have to be replaced. Again, it would be wrong to single out individuals, particularly young William Hague. That would be most unfair!

FINALLY, let us remember all those who suffer from premature hair loss, those who are afflicted with a funny voice, and those whose lives are made difficult by the fact that their girlfriends spell their name in a silly way. (Unlike Cherie! T. B.)

🎄 THE MEANING OF CHRISTMAS 🎄

As Christmas approaches, let us remember the true meaning of Christmas, which is for us all to go out and spend money in the High Street in order to support the economy at this difficult time.

(Not that it is a difficult time, as Mr Brown the Treasurer always reminds us! T.B.)

HYMNS MODERN AND MODERN

(Additional Anthems and Choruses for Parish Use)

NO. 94 **THE ST ALBION PARISH SONG**

> *Life is like a river*
> > *It flows from A to B*
> *It starts off in the mountains*
> > *And goes down to the sea*

(Chorus)
> > *Go with the flow, go with the flow*
> > *Always say 'yes' and never say 'no'*
> > *Go with the flow, go with the flow,*
> > *Look, it's the best idea you know!*

> *Life is like a journey*
> > *It goes from A to Zed*
> *It starts off when you're born*
> > *And ends up when you're dead.*

(Chorus)
> > *Go with the flow, go with the flow*
> > *Always say 'yes' and never say 'no'*
> > *Go with the flow, go with the flow,*
> > *Look, it's the best idea you know!*

(Words T. Blair)

NO. 97 **FOR CHILDREN AT CHRISTMAS**

> *Little Tony, little Tony*
> > *With your heavy load*
> *Little Tony, little Tony*
> > *In the middle of the road*

> *Little Tony, little Tony*
> > *Working every day*
> *Little Tony, little Tony*
> > *To bring us the third way*

(Words Professor Anthony Giddens)

NO. 102 TRADITIONAL XMAS CAROL

The first of May, in ninety-seven
There dawned on the earth the kingdom
of heaven,
The first of May, that was the big night
And ever since then it's all been alright

No way, no way, no way, Hose
We won't forget that glorious day!
No way, no way, no way, Hose
We won't forget that glorious day!

(Words T. Blair)

NO. 103 FOR GENERAL USE

There's a new wind that's blowing
There's a new sky that's bright
There's a new mood at St Albion's
We must be doing things right

There's a new dawn tomorrow
There's a new day today
There's a new mood at St Albion's
Let's make sure it stays that way

(Words T. Blair)

NO. 104 FOR USE AT YOUNG PEOPLES EVENTS

Things are changing, things are moving
Everywhere you go
St Albion's is really swinging
It's where it's at you know.

We must be pivotal and vibrant
Each and every day
We must be modern and relevant
In each and every way.

(Words S. Twigg)

The St Albion's Nativity Play
FULL TEXT

A new, modern and relevant version of the traditional (yawn!) story by Rev. A.R.P. Blair

THE THIRD WAY IN A MANGER

*A*nd it came to pass in a certain country that all the people dwelt in darkness, and were told that they had to go unto their own cities, each one to cast his or her vote. And lo, there was a typical couple — a single mother and a senior citizen who had lost his job under the wicked policies of the previous administration. And on the way to the polling booth, they saw a star shining up above them.

"Look," said Mary. "It is a new dawn!" And Joseph said, "Things can only get better!"

Meanwhile, there were certain poor shepherds demonstrating in the fields about the collapse in farm incomes. And suddenly an angel came unto them.

"Behold," said the angel (or messenger), "I bring you great news. Not about your own situation exactly, because farming comes lower down the list of priorities right now, but really glad tidings all the same. Peace process on earth. Goodwill to all men of violence. That's from the book of Semtex, chapter seven, verse eleven."

Meanwhile, our typical couple came to an inn, looking for somewhere to spend the night.

"Sorry," said the innkeeper. "All the rooms are booked. We've got a delegation of three rich businessmen who've come from the Far East. In fact they got out of the Far East just in time, and sensibly moved their money to the Deutsche Bundesbank. Wise guys."

Anyway, they had booked up all the rooms, so Mary and Joe were told they would have to sleep somewhere else. So, on the day before polling day, things were looking pretty bleak for our couple.

Meanwhile, the rich men had heard news of a "saviour", and they wanted to find him to give him their support. So they came with their gifts of gold, gold and more gold. And notice, nobody kicked up a fuss about them making their donations to such a good cause, saying "Sorry, wise men," — and they must have been wise to have become rich in the first place! — No one said "Sorry, wise men, take your money elsewhere, there's a conflict of interest here!" No way! As it says in the Good Book, "It is easier for a rich man to enter the kingdom of heaven, than a poor man." And talking of poor men, the shepherds went to the polling booth as well to show their support. And the shepherds asked "What can we give, humble, agricultural, working-class folk as we are? We can't give gold like the three rich businessmen. We can't give a lamb, because it's only worth 25p." And they were told they could give something much more valuable. Their vote. Then they were told to get back to their sheep and stop complaining.

So, on the great day everyone gathered round for the big moment when the saviour would come and bring new hope for everybody. It was X-mas you see, the festival when you cast your X.

And what did they find in the polling booth — in the crèche that had been provided for mothers who needed to take their children to vote? They found the message they had all been waiting for! A book called "The Third Way" By Rev. A.R.P. Blair. You see, the "Third Way In A Manger".

ST ALBION PARISH NEWS

25th December 1998

Hullo!

And hasn't it been warm lately? Too warm almost, since it doesn't feel like Christmas and that's very much my theme this week! We all know that Christmas is meant to be a time of peace on earth. But you know, peace doesn't mean not having wars. It doesn't mean people not fighting each other. What sort of peace is that? No, as it says in the good book, "Blessed are the peacemakers, for they shall make war" *(The Good Cruise Bible)*.

You see, peace isn't just a matter of sitting around enjoying ourselves, watching television and eating Mr Sainsbury's excellent mince pies. Thanks, David, for the 200 you sent round to the vicarage! You see, if someone *doesn't* want peace in this world, you have to make them! Obviously, you ask them nicely first! But if they keep on refusing, then you have to warn them! And then, after you've warned them a few more times, eventually you have to give them a punch on the nose!

You see, there are times when you have to stand up to bullies and say enough is enough, you put down your beastly weapons or else!

Though, as Mrs Mowlam has shown, this clearly isn't the right approach in all places. Ireland, for example, is jolly different from the Middle East where all the stories in the Bible are set!

Now, I know some of the older people in the parish have been saying, "Why is the vicar the only one in the world to support his friend the Reverend William Jefferson Clinton, from the Church of the Seven Day Fornicators?" Well, my answer to that is that I am proud to be his friend. He calls me Tony and I call him Mr Clinton. That's the sort of relationship we have. And when I think of him I think of those moving words, "Stand by your man". "Stand by your man." That's from the devotional writings of St Tammy of Wynette.

And that means standing by him, no matter what he's done. Whether in his professional or his private life. Not that Mr Clinton has done anything wrong in his private life. As he himself has been the first to admit, he may have behaved "inappropriately". But that's hardly a sin, is it? There's no commandment saying, "Thou shalt not commit inappropriate behaviour", is there?

And while I'm on the subject of friendship, let me thank all my good friends in the parish who have sent me such lovely Christmas cards.

I particularly liked the one from the first Mrs Cook, showing a traditional Robin surrounded by other birds.

Although I am not sure about the one from our treasurer Mr Brown, saying, "A Merry Christmas and A Not Very Prosperous New Year". I never think funny cards are very appropriate at Christmas!

And talking of not being funny or clever, I certainly don't think much of the card from young Master Hague reading, "I saw Mr Mandelson kissing Santa Claus".

As you know, Cherie and I've been pretty busy recently, planning our holiday and trying to find a chemist who sells suntan lotion at this time of year. So I apologise to anyone whom I may have inadvertently overlooked and not sent a card to in return — like Mr Robinson! For those who didn't get one, here it is, the Family at Christmas.

Yours

Tony

Season's Greetings

Notices

■ Mr Prescott asks you not to bring your cars to our midnight service, but to use public transport instead. He also wants me to remind you that there won't be any buses or trains over the Christmas holiday.

■ The Revd. Ashdown of the United Democratic Reform Church has invited us all to his party. But I've had to make it clear to him that he has to come to *our* party. I'm happy to say he's agreed.

 To Remember In Your Prayers

LET US particularly remember at this time all the old people of our parish, who are struggling to make ends meet, many of them having failed to make adequate provision for their old age when they were younger. Help them to realise that it is all their own fault, and they can't rely on the church for a handout.

LET US also remember the young people, many of whom are struggling to make ends meet, and to find jobs, even though of course there are lots of jobs.
   Help these young people to invest their money wisely in a second pension, remembering the Church's teaching that we should lay up our treasure on earth (*Book of Peps 7.12*).

Holidays. . . . . .

There will be no services in January, as Cherie and I will be taking our usual well-earned break in the Seychelles. £20,000 may seem a lot of money to come out of parish funds for a holiday, but let's not forget "It is better to receive than to give"! I think I've remembered that right!

Also, I don't want to find that people have been squabbling over who will take over while I'm away. I've made it quite clear that Mr Prescott will act as my deputy, but of course Mr Mandelson will be in charge, as normal!

Thank you both! T.B.

ST ALBION PARISH NEWS

8th January 1999

Hullo! And a happy New Year to you all!

You notice I don't say a "Happy Old Year", and that's very much my theme this week!

At the beginning of 1999, we look forward to what is to come, not backwards at unfortunate events which may have happened in the past!

Which is why I won't be dwelling on Mr Mandelson's unexpected resignation as our Churchwarden. Or Mr Robinson's resignation from the PCC. Or Mr Whelan's resignation as Mr Brown's assistant.

I think we all know by now that Peter, through no fault of his own, borrowed some money from his friend Mr Robinson so he could buy himself a nice house.

What's wrong with that, you may ask?

Nothing is the simple answer!

There's nothing in the Good Book that says we can't borrow money from our friends!

After all, didn't Our Lord himself say "Greater love hath no man than this: that he lay out £373,000 for his friend"? *(Revelations 7.16)*

However, Mr Mandelson, being a man of very high principle, knew that he had done nothing wrong, which is why he resigned as our Churchwarden.

But this does not mean that Peter will be leaving the team ministry. No one has played a more important part in revitalising St Albion's and putting our parish on a modern, vital and pivotal footing than Peter (with perhaps one obvious exception, although modesty prevents me from saying who that is!).

Without Peter's vision and hard work, we wouldn't have the Millennium Tent.

It would be just standing there half-finished, with nothing to put in it!

And incidentally, if anyone does have any ideas of what to put in it, could they please send them in asap. But not to Peter obviously, since he's got to be out of action for a while, recharging his batteries!

And if I know my friend Peter, he's not going to be sitting round on the back pews for long, feeling sorry for himself over some supposed "error of judgement" that he never committed in the first place.

As I told Peter, when he stayed with Cherie and me at the vicarage the night after he resigned, "Look, Peter, I want you back at the centre of things, as soon as the dust settles. Although there isn't any dust to settle, obviously!"

And I'm sure everyone in the parish feels the same way! All decent people, that is!

Not those sneerers and snipers who could never understand how much we all owe to Peter — a lot more than the piffling sum he owed to Mr Robinson. "Money can't buy you love," as it says in the *Gospel According To St John, St Paul, St George and St Ringo*!

So, that brings me back to my real message to you all this New Year.

We're going to move forward, looking ahead! And not look back over our shoulders at what may or may not have happened in the past!

Which is why, on New Year's Eve, when Cherie and I and the kids were seeing in the New Year in the Seychelles (largely at our own expense, please note!), I got out my guitar and led them in a chorus, not of *Auld* Lang Syne, but *New* Lang Syne!

Surely that's the right note on which we should all be approaching the New Year and the New Millennium!

Yours,

Peter's friend,

The vicar and Mr Blunkett tell the kids at St Albion Primary how important it is *not* to miss school *(Unless you have a good reason e.g. the vicar is your father and needs an extra few days holiday in the Seychelles).*

MESSAGE FROM THE CHURCHWARDEN, MR MANDELSON

I resign.

PS. I know where you live, Gordon! And I'll get you for this one, if it's the last thing I do. P. M.

Your Letters...

Dear Sir,

Thank goodness we've finally seen the back of that humbugging toady Mr Mandelson with his rich friends and his fancy houses and stupid mobile phones. Can we now get back to some proper, old-fashioned, decent, traditional, honest

Yours sincerely,
J. Prescott,
The Working Men's Club.

As Editor, I reserve the right to cut all letters for reasons of space. A. Campbell

Dear Sir,

I cannot believe that someone so charming as darling Peter can be treated so barbarically and cruelly as though he were some common, ordinary little

Yours faithfully,
Lady Carla Powell,
The Old Thatch Cottage.

Even letters from wealthy supporters of the vicar may have to be edited due to the aforementioned pressures of space. A.C.

✝ To Remember In Your Prayers

Mr Charles Whelan, who had a very difficult Christmas coming to terms with his feelings of guilt over what happened to Mr Mandelson. He may have thought he was being helpful in some way to his friend Mr Brown, our Treasurer, but frankly there are certain things which are more important than loyalty to Mr Brown, and those include loyalty to the vicar of this parish and his friends. Obviously, Mr Whelan did nothing wrong, but he was quite right to resign (even though he took his time!). T.B.

Welcome!

I am delighted to announce that my very old friend Mr Falconer is to take over running the Millennium Tent from my other very old friend Mr Mandelson. Although Charlie has no obvious experience in this line (!) I am sure he will do a wonderful job. So, let's all give him 100% support just like we did to Mr Mandelson before he had to resign for not doing anything wrong. If you want to get Charlie going just ask him round for a coffee and play him some B sides from your old record collection! He's particularly good on the New Riders of the Purple Sage (not the *old* ones obviously!!). And Charlie has already got a great idea for the Millennium Tent. It's a "Sixties Zone". Talk about the Rock and Roll of Ages!

PS. Sorry to Mr Prescott who wanted the job — Charlie just pipped him to the post for this job! Nothing personal! T.B.

ST ALBION PARISH NEWS

22nd January 1999

Hullo!

It's wonderful to start the New Year with some really good news!

Yes, I mean Good News! Not dreary second-hand gossip and tittle-tattle and trivia which nobody is interested in!

"Go ye into the world and proclaim the good news," as it says in St Paul's Letter to the Guardian.

It doesn't say "Go out and tell everyone about your friends' marriage breakdowns. Or which of your friends have been stabbing each other in the back." No, it doesn't! Even if all these things are true, which they aren't! And even if they were, it wouldn't be important.

No, the important thing is to move on and to get on with our great mission — which is to spread the good news that we at St Albion's are a united happy team, working together for a common aim!

So, let's take no notice of Mrs Cook. Not the delightful Gaynor, of course, whom we see in church every week turning the pages for her husband in the organ loft!

No, the one I mean is Mr Cook's former wife who sadly has been going round telling anyone who will listen about the sad details of her marriage.

Look, I'm not suggesting that Margaret has made it all up! That would be unfair, though we all know that middle-aged women often suffer from a mid-life crisis where they drink too much and have hallucinations.

So, Margaret, my advice to you, on behalf of all our congregation, would be to start a new life somewhere else, as far away as possible from all the things that you have imagined have happened here!

In the spirit of forgiveness, I suggest you move to New Zealand and don't upset yourself by returning here ever again. (With the "thirty pieces of silver" you received from the St Albion's Examiner, you can surely afford it!)

So enough of Mrs Cook, who would do well to remember that ancient text "If you have nothing nice to say about someone, then surely it is better to say nothing" *(Book of Clichés, 23.12)*.

Look, I'll be frank. I've got nothing nice to say about Margaret, so I'm not going to waste the whole of this newsletter going on about what a fool she is making of herself, and how she would have done much better just to concentrate on what a first-class job her ex-husband is doing for the parish!

But anyway, that's quite enough about Mrs Cook. Although there is one more point that could be made, which is that she might remember the parable of *The Woman Whose Husband Was Taken In Adultery*.

And what happened to her? She got stoned to death! And in my view quite right too!

Yours in Chrisis,

Tony

A LETTER FROM THE EX-CHURCHWARDEN, MR MANDELSON

Dear Tony,

I wondered if I could use the columns of the parish news to clear up some confusion about my recent resignation. It seems that some people are suggesting that I am not sorry enough about what happened. I name no names, but Mr Prescott and Mr Brown will know who I am talking about! I would like to make it clear that I am very sorry indeed for the way these people have failed to understand that I did nothing wrong and that, in retrospect, I perhaps acted a little too hastily in resigning. P.M.

(Quite right, Peter! That's put the record straight! And I would like to make it clear that even though you are no longer Churchwarden, you are still my "personal representative" in the parish. T.B.)

The Editor reserves the right to print all letters in full when they are written by friends of Tony. A.C.

Thought For The Day

"The wages of spin is death"

Book of Lost Job

(Sent in by Mr Livingstone, proprietor of our local aquatic pet centre Newts R Us)

A MESSAGE FROM MR DOBSON
Director of the St Albion's Hospice

Contrary to what certain ill-informed people have been putting around in the Britannia Arms, there is no shortage of nursing staff in our hospice during the current 'flu epidemic (which incidentally is not an epidemic by any stretch of the imagination, even though everyone seems to have gone down with it!).

We have plenty of nurses here, many of whom have come over from their homes in the Philippines to help us out. And for those of you who say we can't afford them, let me assure you that these girls cost only six times more than their English equivalents, which makes them real value for money, as I am sure our Treasurer Mr Brown would agree! F.D.

(Well done, Frank! T.B.)

The Story Of The Man Who Was Saved

And one day, when the disciples were out fishing, one of them said, "Master, there is a Danish tourist drowning over there. What shall we do?" And he said unto them, "I shall go and rescue him forthwith," walking on the water as he did so. And when the man was brought forth from the water, he cried "What is all the fuss about? I was just out for a swim, and waving to my wife who was on the shore."

The Moral:
There's no pleasing some people! T.B.

Notices

■ The vicar will be giving a talk in the church hall on Monday evening, entitled **"Not Upper Class or Lower Class but Middle Class — The Third Way Again"**. (This is obviously *not* a relaunch of my mission, because my mission does not need relaunching! T.B.)

■ The new Church Warden, Dr Cunningham, has suggested replacing the annual wine 'n' cheese do with a weekly **"Champagne and Caviar"** party in the Vestry. Any thoughts? T.B.

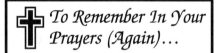

✝ To Remember In Your Prayers (Again)...

Our good friend the Rev. William Jefferson Clinton III from the Church of the Seven Day Fornicators, whose flock are at this very moment taking a vote on whether to de-frock him (something they claim he has been doing to various ladies in his congregation). Like Mr Cook, the Rev. Clinton has done a marvellous job, and it really is time for everybody to stop going on about his private life, which is entirely his affair (not that it was an affair, as he has been the first to point out!). Let us pray, therefore, that his people will come to their senses and learn how to move on. T.B.

ST ALBION PARISH NEWS

5th February 1999

Hullo!

I hope you are all keeping well and have managed to keep this flu at bay! It's no laughing matter, as I saw for myself when I made an unannounced visit to our local hospital, St Aneurin's!

It was very heartwarming to see the dedication of the nurse, as she coped splendidly with the hundreds of patients who were queuing up for admission!

There can't be much wrong with a hospital where people are prepared to wait for 18 hours just to get in!

As the nurse told me, with a smile, "People are literally dying to get in here!"

As I came away, I couldn't help thinking how impressive was the dedication of that nurse — someone in a responsible position, serving the public without any thought of financial reward!

I expect all of you can think of somebody like that! I know I can! Someone standing not very far from you who is actually foregoing any increase in his vicar's stipend, as an example to others around him who put wages before service.

I don't want to bring personalities into this, but Mr Prescott will know who I might be referring to! No offence, John, but you don't get tipped working as a steward for the parish, you know!

As it says in the Bible, "Blessed are the do-gooders. For they shall hunger and thirst because they aren't paid anything" *(Sermon on the Cheap, Matthew 8.13)*.

What a lesson for us all! You see, we mustn't go on about money, as if it was the only thing which matters!

Look, some people will always be poor, like nurses, teachers and the like.

And some people will always be rich, like our friends Mr Robinson, Mr Sainsbury and Mr Murdoch.

The difference is that the ones who are poor get their reward in terms of our esteem and gratitude, and the knowledge that they are contributing something really valuable to the community.

But so, of course, are the rich people! Thank goodness we've moved on from the days when it was thought to be a crime to make money and that there was something admirable about not making any!

Yours,

Tony

IMPORTANT ANNOUNCEMENT

■ The Vicar wishes it to be known that he is extremely angry over criticism in the parish of his decision to send his daughter Antonia not to St Albion's Primary School but the Convent of the Sacred League Tables in the neighbouring parish of Richman-on-Thames. I would like to remind everyone that I could easily send my children to private schools if I so wished. But I prefer to stand by my principles and to send Antonia to the best school that money can't buy. Anyone else could do exactly the same, if they were the vicar. As it says in the Good Book, "Many are called, but very few get in, including mine" *(Book of Strings, Ch.5)*.

NEW CHORUS

**For use in next Sunday's Evensong.
Try to learn the word's everyone —**
Jack Cunningham, Church Warden.

The bad old days are over,
We can't live in the past,
We're not upper, we're not lower,
No, we're now all middle class.

Chorus

*Middle class, middle class,
That's what we are today,
Middle class, middle class,
It's the Thi-ird Way!*   **(Words and music T. Blair)**

MOVING ON...

Our best wishes to the Rev Ashdown of the United Reform Democratic Church who has sadly decided to step down and retire with Jane to Yeovil. Enjoy yourself, Paddy. You deserve a good long rest after all the work you have done in working to bring your church closer to mine! We all want our oecumenical "project" to succeed, and I am sure that your successor, the Rev Kennedy (if that's who your congregation is sensible enough to choose!) will carry on the good work!

T.B.

Parish Postbag...

Dear Vicar,

Let us hope that the departure of the Rev Pantsdown will finally knock on the head all this bloody silly talk about unity between the churches. We at St Albion's can do perfectly well on our own, thank you very much, without any help from

Yours faithfully,
J. Prescott,
The Working Men's Club.

The Editor continues to reserve the right to cut all letters from Mr Prescott. A.C.

Dear Sir,

It's all very well for the vicar to tell the rest of the PCC to go without their pay rises. But not all of us have got a rich wife who ponces around the law courts in a stupid wig earning millions of pounds defending lesbians who want to

Yours faithfully,
John Prescott,
The Working Men's Club.

The Editor continues to reserve the right to cut all letters from Mr Prescott. A.C.

ST ALBION PARISH NEWS

19th February 1999

Hullo!

Once again, Lent is upon us. And I hope you all enjoyed Mr Sainsbury's "genetically modified" pancakes at the church hall! I certainly did!

But Lent is really a time to concentrate our thoughts on the things that really matter! It's a time when we try to empty our lives of trivia!

Not an easy thing to do these days, when we are surrounded by the outpourings of the media and their obsession with mindless chat shows, pop stars, football — and TV soap operas!

But we must do better than that! That is why earlier this week I took the opportunity to appear on our local radio station, Albion FM, and put across some serious points to all the listeners to the popular Johnny Jackson "Coffee Break Show".

Mr Campbell, the editor of this newsletter, kindly suggested that instead of me rambling on, we should just publish a transcript of my interview (unedited!) for those parishioners who may have missed it.

JJ: *Hi, Vicar, great to have you back! What a great track there from Pink Floyd!*

TB: *Too right, JJ, I've got the album and I was playing it only the other day!*

JJ: *Now, we promised to talk about the big issues on this prog. So, let's kick off with the really big one. What do we think about Glenn Hoddle? Our phone-in shows that people think he should go.*

TB: *Do they? Well, in that case, I think he should go too! Assuming he said those things, which I am sure he did!*

JJ: *We can't have people believing in all that religious clap-trap in this day and age, can we?*

TB: *Yeah, look, I mean it's the 21st Century, isn't it, JJ?*

JJ: *Stay with us, Vicar, we're just going to take a short break for today's recipe from Marge Watkins, St Albion's Microwave Gourmet!*

(Recipe omitted. A.C.)

TB: *Mmm. I fancy a bit of that! Sounds delicious! Salmon and broccoli quiche has always been my favourite! And Cherie's too!*

JJ: *That's funny! Last time you were on, you said your favourite was tripe and onions.*

TB: *Ha ha ha!*

JJ: *But, seriously, we've had a lot of really sad news this week. It's been death and gloom all round, hasn't it?*

TB: *Sure. When a really great man passes on, someone who's been loved by millions, then we all feel a personal sense of loss.*

JJ: *You knew the King personally, I believe?*

TB: *No, I meant Alf Roberts from the Street.*

JJ: *He died in real life as well, you know.*

TB: *Did he? Well, that's doubly sad! I am sure all your listeners would like to join me in a moment's prayer.*

JJ: *That's a great idea, Vicar. And while we're all praying, let's listen to something from Boyzone.*

(Track omitted. A.C.)

I think you'll all agree that my appearance on JJ's Show helped to put Lent into perspective, and gave all of you something serious to think about during the 40 days and nights before we have a chance to get at one of those delicious genetically modified chocolate Easter eggs from our friend Mr Sainsbury's shop!

> Yours,
>
> Tony

!!CONGRATULATIONS!!

Our happy thoughts go out to my old friend William Jefferson Clinton of the Church of the Seven Day Fornicators. His flock have decided not to defrock him after all and have found that he was innocent of everything — even the adultery and the lying which he has confessed to! Good for Bill, this proves my instincts about people are always right! T.B.

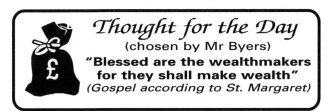

Thought for the Day
(chosen by Mr Byers)
"Blessed are the wealthmakers for they shall make wealth"
(Gospel according to St. Margaret)

St Albion's Honoured In Poll!

A recent opinion poll asked people living in our area which individual in the world today they most looked up to as a spiritual and moral leader. The results were as follows:

1. Rev. A.R.P. Blair, Vicar of St Albion's

2. His Holiness The Dalai Lama

3. His Holiness The Pope

4. The Late Mother Teresa

5. The Late Diana, Princess of Wales

6. Nelson Mandela

7. Glenn Hoddle

8. Mystic Meg

9. Trevor McDonald

10. H.M. The Queen

TB writes: This makes me feel very humble and proud! It is a tribute to everyone at St Albion's that they have chosen the most widely respected spiritual leader in the world to be their vicar!"

✝ Lenten Round Up ✝

We asked some of our better-known parishioners to say what they are giving up for Lent.

✝ *Mr Mandelson: "I shall be giving up my job and my house. In a sense, I am giving up for Lent what I have been lent!"*

(TB writes: He may have lost his house, but it is good to see that Peter hasn't lost his sense of humour! You won't be long in "the wilderness", Peter, I'm sure!)

✝ *Mr Lairg: "I am giving up wearing silly old-fashioned clothes in church."*

(TB: Quite right, Derry. Let's give up the old-fashioned ideas with them!)

✝ *Mr Cunningham: "I am giving up travelling first-class on parish business. In future, I will only be using the Diamond Executive Club Class."*

(TB: That's a big sacrifice, Jack! Perhaps our friend Gordon could follow your example!)

✝ *Mr Adams: "I am giving up nothing. Is that clear?"*

(TB: I am sure Gerry doesn't mean this literally!)

✝ *Mrs Mowlam: "I am giving up."*

(TB: I think we all have that feeling sometimes, Mo. But, remember, when things look really black, I'm always here to help sort them out!)

ST ALBION PARISH NEWS

5th March 1999

Hullo!

I can only have one theme this week, and that is the importance of unity, which means no one being left out and everyone being left in!

Like with our "parish changeover plan", to start taking the collection in Euros like our fellow churches on the Continent instead of old-fashioned pounds!

You know, when everybody wants to do one thing, because it is a sensible idea, then the person who thinks they want to do something else looks pretty silly!

I don't want to mention any names but I think we're all agreed that Mr William Hague from the 6th Form Debating Society has made a bit of a fool of himself recently.

As it says in the Good Book, "He who is not with me, is against me" *(Letter to the Euromans 2.16).*

If we just stand on the sidelines being negative, how can we hope to play any part in building a better world?

When I visited the local swimming pool recently I saw one little lad, shivering on the side and refusing to go in.

"Why won't you go in and join the others?" I asked him.

"Because I can't swim, Vicar," the boy replied.

"Well, if you don't take the plunge, you'll never learn," I told him, and gave him a good push to help him on his way.

With the help of the lifeguard, he was soon back on the side, with no harm done!

But the important thing was that he had learned a very useful lesson, which is that, if we ever want to achieve anything in this life, we must always be ready to join in.

Yours,

Tony

✝ To Remember In Your Prayers

Mr Rhodri Morgan, who was very disappointed at not being appointed conductor of our Welsh Male Voice Choir. It may be that most people in the choir wanted him to get the job, but that is hardly the point. The important thing is whoever is chosen should be someone who can work closely with the Vicar, and make sure that they can all sing from the same hymn sheet without any wrong notes. That is why the choir chose my friend Mr Michael.

So we therefore pray that Mr Morgan may be guided to remain silent on this matter, rather than going around the parish whingeing that the whole thing was rigged. T.B.

Notices From The Editor, A. Campbell

I would like to make it clear that there is nothing peculiar about the fact that, as Editor of the Parish Newsletter, I attend all meetings of the PCC. I do this on the personal invitation of the Vicar, whom I happen to know greatly values my input.

However, the idea that I would presume to tell the Vicar how to run the parish is absurd. I merely make suggestions, which he then acts upon, much as Mr Mandelson used to do before he had to go on his sabbatical.

I hope this will put an end to the tittle-tattle in the Cool Britannia Arms. A.C.

Millennium Tent Update

from Mr Falconer ("Charlie")

It has not been easy stepping into Mr Mandelson's shoes at this late stage, but I think I've come up with a pretty exciting list of suggestions for how we can make the Tent a great success. These include:

● special Millennium Tent pencils with the words "St Albion's 2000"

● special car stickers reading "We've seen the Tent. Have you?"

● special tea towels printed with a full colour black-and-white photo of the Vicar, with caption "St Albion's Man of the Millennium!"

We hope that most of these items will be "on line" in time for the ceremonial opening of the Tent in July 2001. *(Is this right? A.C.)*

Looking Ahead...

It may seem a long time ahead to next summer's Flower Festival, but I know that some of you are already making preparations for the vegetable section. Our good friend Mr Sainsbury tells me that he is quietly confident of winning all the categories. He tells me, "My tomatoes are already the size of a football, my marrow weighs three tons and my carrots are unbelievable. They've got birds' wings, fish heads and they're bright blue!"

We won't ask David what is his secret, because that's very much his business! But we're all really looking forward to seeing them! T.B.

Parish Postbag

Dear Vicar,

Contrary to some predictions (ie, yours!), there was a really big turn-out in the Church Hall, when I asked people to support my campaign to play the part of Lord Mayor of London in the St Albion's pantomime. Can you imagine that amount of people turning out to hear you giving one of your ser

> *Yours sincerely,*
> *K. Livingstone,*
> *Newts R Us (The Aquatic*
> *Pet Centre), The High St.*

(The Editor reserves the right to cut any letter from Mr Livingstone for reasons of space. A.C.)

SPECIAL SERVICE FOR RACIAL HARMONY IN THE PARISH

The Vicar writes:

 The last thing any of us want to do is jump on the bandwagon surrounding the tragic story of poor Stephen Lawrence, which is why I am holding a special service next Sunday to express our solidarity with our local black community. So, if anyone knows any black people, please ask them along!

HYMNS MODERN AND MODERN

(Additional Anthems and Choruses for Parish Use)

NO. 95 **FOR USE IN THE SUNDAY SCHOOL**

Tell us the message, tell us the message
Tell us the message, please
I'll tell you the message
It's the one-two-three E-E's!

(Chorus)

Education, education, education
Everybody sing
Education, education, education,
That's the vital thing

Yes, that is our message
Whether it's free or you're paying fees
Yes that is the message
It's the one-two-three E-E's

(Chorus)

(Words D. Blunkett)

NO. 105 **CHORUS FOR LADIES FOCUS GROUPS**

When the night is black
And the clouds are grey
There is always one thing
that we can confidently say:

Tony is our beacon, shining in the dark
Tony is our beacon, shining in the dark
Tony is our beacon, shining in the dark

Shine Tony Shine
Shine Tony Shine

(Words Mrs C. Short)

ST ALBION PARISH NEWS

19th March 1999

Hullo!

It's nice to see Mr Brown getting so much richly deserved praise for his annual presentation of the church's finances!

And how pleased we all were to see the annual picture of him and Miss Macaulay together in the local paper!

Gordon tells me he is very keen on "the family". But I had to point out to him that, even these days, it is usual to get married first before having one! (Though not essential — it's important not to be judgemental on these matters — as we all know, it is equally valid to have a meaningful relationship with a partner, same sex or otherwise, or indeed not to have a partner at all!)

I would like to be the first to congratulate Gordon for doing everything I suggested to balance the books. Well done!

But before people get too carried away in hailing Gordon as some kind of a genius, over a few drinks in the Cool Britannia Arms, we must remember that Gordon is a member of a team, as he would be the first to acknowledge (I hope!).

So if he is tempted to feel pleased with himself, which I am sure he won't, he would do well to remember that it is the team which has done well. The real credit must go to the leader of the team, whoever that may be!

Because the leader is the person who picks the team. So people like Gordon would be nowhere if it wasn't for the person who chose him in the first place!

Didn't we all sing that wonderful chorus at last Sunday's Youth Service?

> *"I am the leader, the leader,*
> *the leader of the gang*
> *I am."*

(Words and Music G.Glitter, arr. T.Blair)

So let's hear no more about "Flash Gordon" or "The Scottish Wizard"!

I'm sure Gordon would be the first to admit that this kind of silly adulation is extremely unhelpful and very much against the spirit of St.Albion's, which is to give credit where it is really due!

Your friend and Saviour

Tony *(Not Gordon!)*

52

A POSTCARD FROM MR. PRESCOTT

We received the following postcard from Mr.Prescott of the Working Men's Club, who has been on a two week fact-finding holiday in India. He writes:

As you can see, the missus and I are taking a leaf out of your book, Tony, and skiving off on an all-expenses-paid

This postcard has had to be cut for reasons of space. A.Campbell, Editor.

TEXT OF THE WEEK

(chosen by Mr Gordon Brown)

"The Lord giveth and the Lord taketh away — often at the same time without you noticing it."

Book of Miras, 7.13

✝ To Remember In Your Prayers

Our very good friends the Rev. William Jefferson Clinton of the Church of the Seven Day Fornicators and his future ex-wife Hillary, who are facing a bit of a rocky patch in their marriage (or not as the case may be, it's not really any of our business after all!). Anyway, let us pray that Hillary will learn to follow the example of the Blessed Tammy of Wynette, who taught us to "Stand by your Man" and warned us of the perils of "D.I.V.O.R.C.E"!

We also remember Cathy Woodhead, the former wife of our popular school inspector Chris. May she learn the virtue of silence. It really doesn't help to drag up the past, as if it had some relevance to the great work that Chris has been doing with the Sixth-formers at St Albion's School for girls. She could learn from the mistakes of Margaret Cook, who has become a laughing stock in the parish for spreading rumours about Robin, in an effort to undermine his very happy new marriage to Gaynor. I am sorry, Margaret, but as you may realise from Robin's high standing in the parish, he's had the last laugh! T.B.

Verses From A Local Businessman

Contributed by M.Heseltine

Although I am not a regular member of his congregation, I would like to commend the Rev. A.R.P. Blair for his sensible stand on closer links with our European friends.

P.S. I am obviously not much of a poet but I am a very busy man and I have not got time to think out a lot of silly rhymes. The important thing is to annoy that little squit William Hague from the sixth form debating society.

MH, The Huge House,
Tarzan Crescent.

RECIPE OF THE DAY

Sent in by Mr Michael (Conductor of the St Albion's Welsh Male Voice Choir)

Beef-Off-The-Bone

Ingredients:

1 Bone
1 Plate of Beef

Instructions:

Place beef in mouth.
Then deny eating it.

Tips:

Serves no-one

Thanks, Alan! TB

ST ALBION PARISH NEWS

2nd April 1999

Hullo!

A rather grim hullo this week, as our thoughts are all on the tragic events in Kosovo!

For those of you who don't know where that is, Mr Cook, our geography expert, has made a little map *(see below)*.

As you can see, this place Kosovo is not very near St Albion's.

But that doesn't mean that it's nothing to do with us. I was standing in the check-out queue at Tesco's only yesterday, when one parishioner came up to me and said, "Vicar, I listened to your sermon last week about Mr Slobovich, I think it was. But I thought we were meant to turn the other cheek in these situations?"

"You're quite right," I said, "we should do that. But then we should turn round and give whoever it is a really good thump. 'For that is the only language that such people understand,' as it says in the Old Testament *(First Book of Cabbies, 18.40 plus tip)*. That's the way we have to deal with bullies."

But our Tesco friend refused to see my point. "I'm sorry, Vicar, I disagree," he said.

I had to remind him that I was the Vicar, and that I knew best! I tried negotiating with him for some minutes. But when he refused to accept my final warning, I had no alternative but to push him into a large stack of baked bean cans, which collapsed all over his head! (I'm sorry about the elderly lady who tripped over one of the cans and broke her hip, but as it says in the Book of Proverbs, 'You can't make an omelette without breaking legs'!)

I am sure this is a lesson our Tesco friend won't forget in a hurry! And the same goes for our Serbian friend Mr Milosevich.

That's why this Sunday we will end our service with a rousing chorus of "Onward Christian Bombers" (No. 94, *Hymns Modern & Modern*).

And now to events nearer home! I have decided to abolish child poverty, which must be good news for everyone! (Our Tesco friend, please note — at least one of us is trying to do something constructive!)

And, of course, you can't abolish child poverty without abolishing poverty!

So, that's it! All poverty will be gone!

It looks as if Our Lord was being a little short-sighted when he said, "The poor will be always with you"!

But then it is only fair to remember that He was living in the past, a long time ago, and could not be expected to look forward to the St Albion's of today.

A Happy Easter to you all (and that even includes my Tesco friend!).

Tony

Verses From A Local Poet

Spring In Cumbria

I wandered lonely as a cloud
And breathed in deep the fresh spring air
And all at once I began to smile
As my thoughts turned to our vicar, the
Reverend A.R.P. Blair!

Melvyn (Lord) Bragg,
Ullswater Road.

Who says the Arts are in trouble in this parish? Great stuff, Melvyn! T.B.

✝ To Remember In Your Prayers

Joe Ashton, who is well-known in the parish, especially for the charitable work he does among the deprived girls at the Thai-Me-Up refuge. We pray that malicious tongues will soon be silent, when it comes to passing on irresponsible rumours about what Mr Ashton was up to.

What Mr Ashton wants to do in the privacy of a massage parlour is entirely his own affair and that of the police. Enough said?

Miss Fiona Jones, who has let down herself and St Albion's very badly indeed by her dishonesty over the arrangements for the PCC elections. I find Fiona's behaviour quite unforgiveable, as I am sure you will too. As it says in the story of *The Woman Taken In Adulteration of her Election Expenses*, "Let he who is without a stone, go and get one and then throw it at her."

PASSING THOUGHTS...

A sad farewell to my old friend Mr Ernie Wise, whom I never met but whose programmes Cherie and I used to watch with enormous pleasure. "Bring me sunshine." How true that is! And who has ever expressed the spirit of Christmas better than Little Eric! T.B.

LETTERS TO THE EDITOR

Dear Vicar,

As your father-in-law, I have a better right than most to criticise your way of doing things — ie, not allowing a free and frank expression of

Yours faithfully,
Tony Booth,
C/o The Old Boozer,
The High Street.

The editor reserves the right to cut letters for reasons of space. A.C.

TEXT OF THE WEEK

(chosen by Mr George Robertson)

"Blessed are the warmakers for they shall make peace"
(Acts of the Optimists, 17.3)

ST ALBION PARISH NEWS

16 April 1999

Hullo!

And, contrary to what you may have heard about your vicar being tired and worn out by my duties, I have never felt more wide awake in my entire trousers.

Where was I? Yes, hullo everyone! And let's hear no more of this rubbish about me being exhausted through overwork.

As you can see, I am wide asleep and raring for bed. As it says in the Good Book, "The leopard shall lie down with the lamb and have a jolly good kip." That's from the *Book of Bedtime*, and I think we can all learn a lot from it.

Yes, it's true, I have been busy, working for peace in different parts of the world. And I'm perfectly well aware that, so far, there is rather more war than peace going on.

But that's only to be expected. And I did expect it, even though I didn't mention it to you in my last newsletter, because I didn't want to depress anyone.

"But have you thought this through, Vicar?" I'm always being asked, particularly by our friend in Tesco, who seems to wait for me there by the checkout just to ask me some, frankly, rather silly questions.

"Did you really think this one through, Vicar?" he asked. "Of course I did," I told him, trying to be polite.

"Then you knew it would be a complete balls-up?" he replied. Unfortunately, at this point, my interrogator somehow fell over backwards into the frozen desserts cabinet where he remained for some time.

So, you see, I am fighting fit, and not at all tired. If I was tired, I might be irritable and lose my temper, and push people into freezer cabinets for asking silly questions about a war which is none of their business.

But, fortunately, I am not at all tired, and am looking forward to Easter.

Talking of Easter (and, incidentally, well done all the ladies for the marvellous flowers in the church!), some of you have asked me what our mission to Northern Ireland achieved at our recent very important meeting.

Well, thanks to a lot of hard talking by Mo (and myself!), everyone on all sides agreed that we would definitely go away and think very hard about the need for agreement.

You can't get more positive than that!

So, that's my message to you all this Christmas. Let's sleep on it, shall we?

Goodnight!

Tony

 The vicar, looking not at all tired, wishes all his parishioners "A Happy Eater"!

WELCOME BACK...

We are very happy to welcome back into the fold Mr Sarwar, who had some problems with the police, but has now been completely exonerated. Let me say that I personally always believed in his innocence, even though obviously I had to ban him from the church and ask parishioners temporarily not to shop at his store. T.B.

Parish Postbag

Dear Sir,

    As someone who fought in the last war (unlike some young whippersnappers I could name), I was appalled by our vicar's warmongering sermon at Evensong last week. Surely, even someone as naive as he appears to be can appreciate how absolutely
        Yours sincerely,
        Denis Healey,
        British Legion,
        Anzio Drive.

Dear Sir,

    If our church stands for anything, it is surely peace and brotherhood. How exactly does bombing the
        Yours faithfully,
        T. Benn,
        The Old Quakery,
        Teabag Road.

The editor reserves the right to cut letters for treasons of space. A.C.

Verses From A Local Poet

Come friendly bombs
    and fall on Belgrade.

Isn't that how peace is
        made?

Alistair Campbell
(no relation)

Parish Football

Many thanks to local businessman Mr Murdoch for his generous offer to sponsor our local Albion squad, which I have had to turn down. I know that Mr Murdoch seems to think that I agreed to this proposal (he has even had the team shirts made up with "Murdoch Adult Mags 'n' Vids" printed on them), but he must have misunderstood me. Perhaps the former churchwarden, Mr Mandelson, told him that the deal was done by mistake, but I certainly didn't! In fact, the first I heard about it was when I had to tell Mr Murdoch that his offer, though marvellous in its way, was not really appropriate at the moment. "We can't have one man running everything in the whole parish," I told him, "unless it's me." T.B.

ST ALBION PARISH NEWS

30th April 1999

Hullo!

Once again, sad to say, there is only one subject for me to write about this week — and that is the attempts to bring peace to the poor people of Kosovo.

St Albion Parish News — The Paper That Supports Our Bombs!

You would have thought that there was not much room for disagreement on this one. Surely everybody is in favour of peace, which means they must also be in favour of the war!

Wasn't it Our Lord who said "I come not to bring peace, immediately, but the sword, for as long as it takes. And then peace." *(Letter To the Macedonians, 7.12, Revised [again] Version)*

Some of you asked me, after my sermon last week, "But, Vicar, is this a just war?"

To which my answer is, of course it is a just war! Just take time out for a moment, to remember what the Church Fathers laid down all those years ago.

This is what that great Anglo-Saxon abbot St Ealth of Bomba had to say in the early 11th Century, in his famous treatise *De Justo Bello*:

1. A war is just when it is fought for a just cause.

2. A war is just when it is fought against men who are not just.

3. A war is just so long as no civilians are hurt (except, of course, by the kind of accident which is unfortunately sometimes unavoidable in times of a just war).

4. A war is just so long as ground troops are not committed, unless they can enter Kosovo unopposed. *(I am paraphrasing a bit here, but St Ealth's meaning is pretty clear!)*

So, you see, there really isn't any room for argument here, as I told our friend in Tesco's, who was once again waiting to accost me at the 8 Items Or Less checkout.

"Ah, Vicar," he said. "I see you are stocking up. Are you expecting it's going to go nuclear?"

"These kind of comments are not very helpful at such a difficult time," I told him, "when it behooves all of us to keep calm and collected."

So saying, our argumentative friend unfortunately tripped over my outstretched foot and fell rather heavily into a display of Easter eggs marked "All at half price".

As I later explained at the meeting of the Irish Mission to St Gerry's, the important thing is that everyone should agree even if they have different opinions.

"We're not going to get anywhere," I told them, "if everyone comes up with different ideas about the way forward."

Which is why I suggested that we should all take time out for a period of quiet reflection lasting a good few months, and then come back and look at it all again in a new light, from a different angle and in a fresh perspective.

That way we can look forward to a time of real peace, in Northern Ireland, Kosovo and everywhere else in the world.

Surely we can all agree on that?

Yours,

NATONY

Some of the refugees we haven't found room for. Sorry, this is a small parish, lets face it! T.B.

An Unfortunate Incident

The Vicar writes: I was very sorry to hear that some parishioners made hurtful and wounding comments about the way Mr Prescott of the Working Men's Club took last week's meeting of the PCC during my unavoidable absence on very important parish business. Just because Mr Prescott got muddled up when he was asked some simple questions, got Christmas confused with Easter and asked for "Any Other Business" at the beginning of the meeting rather than the end, this does not justify people complaining that he is a mentally deficient imbecile who is quite unfit to exercise a position of responsibility in the parish!! T.B.

From The Postbag

Dear Sir,
What on earth is happening in this parish? I turn up to church hoping to hear a sermon expounding the traditional beliefs of our church in peace at all costs and an opposition to imperialist warmongering by neo-Colonialist aggressors such as
Yours sincerely,
Mrs Gwyneth Dunwoody,
Aldermaston Road.

Mr Campbell, the Editor of the Newsletter, reserves the right to cut all letters for reasons of space. He also reserves the right to be absent for the next few weeks since he has been headhunted to edit the NATO in-house newsletter "War Cry". A.C.

St Albion's Primary School

From Mr Blunkett, Chairman of the Governors

I want to put it on record that I have every faith in our inspector Chris Woodhead, who is doing a first-class job in improving educational standards.

It is highly regrettable that his former wife, egged on by certain malcontents, has dredged up an incident from many years ago which has no bearing at all on Chris's ability to carry out his present duties. Chris assures me that all these unhelpful allegations are completely untrue — and I believe him. An educational inspector of his calibre knows all about pupils and making "passes". D.B.

ST ALBION PARISH NEWS

14 May 1999

Hullo!

And a very special *hullo!* this week to all the seven Kosovan refugees whom we have welcomed to the parish as our contribution to solving the tragic temporary problems of the Balkans until, of course, the war is won and they can return safely to what remains of their homes!

As you probably know, our Kosovan friends have been put up in the old St Albion's gasworks, which has been converted over the weekend by the ladies of the parish.

I think this open-hearted gesture proves all those people wrong who said that St Albion's shouldn't take in any of the refugees.

How ridiculous! Particularly hurtful was the comment of our friend in Tesco's, who was once again waiting for me at the checkout last week, even suggesting that I should donate some of the contents of my trolley to the new refugees.

I pointed out that our visitors would have no use for such items as kiwi fruit, sun-dried tomatoes or New Zealand Chardonnay. "I thought you said we weren't going to take them in," said our argumentative friend, "because it sent 'the wrong signals' to Mr Milosevic. Now you say it's our duty to offer them sanctuary. You don't know what you are doing, Vicar, do you?"

"I know exactly what I am doing," I told him, as he inexplicably fell face first into a reduced price over-ripe camembert. As he climbed out of the deli counter, covered in stinking cheese, our friend looked distinctly shaken. Perhaps, like Mr Milosevic, he is beginning to crumble, and he will soon be suing for peace!

Elsewhere in this issue you will find a report of my hugely successful visit to Macedonia by our editor Mr Campbell. I would have written about it myself, but modesty forbids!

Yours,

Tony

TEXT OF THE WEEK

Chosen by the Rev. Natony Blair

"And if your left foot should offend you, then shoot yourself in it at once."

Book of (Chinese) Proverbs, 7.15.

St Albion's in the Balkans!

"War Be With You" The Vicar Tells His New Flock

Our Vicar was given an ecstatic welcome by more than half a million refugees when he made a surprise mercy visit to Macedonia last week. Many of them had walked hundreds of miles to greet him, and it was an emotional moment for them when they at last saw the man about whom they had heard so much. The Vicar preached an eloquent sermon on the theme of "the just war, so long as it is just in the air". Although they didn't understand every word he said, the refugees were deeply moved to another refugee camp down the road. A.C.

Good Manners

*I understand that once again parishioners have been making fun of Mr Prescott of our Working Men's Club for mispronouncing foreign names and getting his words mixed up when standing in for the Vicar. When he read out prayers for "Kostobrava" and then announced that "Service will be served after the coffee in the vestibule", this was **not** funny, and it is bad manners to mock someone just because he has not had the benefit of a private education, like the Vicar. T.B.*

Suggestions Box

One of our parishioners has come up with an excellent idea to stop us giving offence to all the Sikhs and Muslims in the parish every time we refer to the date. He suggests that in future we replace the old offensive AD and BC with something that people of all creeds can live happily with, ie BT and AT — "Before Tony" and "After Tony". That makes today's date 12 May 0002AT!

PARISH POSTBAG

Dear Vicar,
*   You stupid, irresponsible twat! You and your friend the Rev. Clinton are talking out of your bums. You are worse than Hitler. Worse even than Nixon. Your hands are covered in*
*   Yours sincerely,*
*   Harold Pinter, Caretaker,*
*   Magnesia Lodge,*
*   Sidcup Road.*

The Editor reserves the right to shorten letters for reasons of space or obscenity. A. Campbell

+ + + + + + Notices + + + + + +

■ I was very disappointed to hear of the very poor turn-out for my friend Professor Giddens's lecture on **"The Globalisation Of World Internationalism"**. Four people really is a poor show for such an important talk, particularly when two of those people were Cherie and myself, and the other two were Mrs Giddens and her friend Mrs Wainwright. Do please make an effort to attend his next talk, on **"The Internationalising Of World Globalisation"**, or Mr Cunningham, the Churchwarden, will come round and do some of his enforcing!

■ I was also very disappointed by the even poorer turn-out to select team leaders for the new self-governing **Scottish Country Dancing Group** and the **Independent Welsh Male (and Female) Voice Choir**. If no one is bothered about choosing the leaders, I might as well choose them myself!

Luckily my friends Mr Dewar and Mr Michael won enough votes to take over these new societies, but I have to say that the lack of gratitude displayed was pretty hurtful.

T.B.

ST ALBION PARISH NEWS

28 May 1999

Hullo!

And once again I am writing to you from the St Albion's Mission in Macedonia, where I have had yet another wonderful welcome from all the refugees.

I can't tell you how it helps me to keep parish affairs in perspective to come out here once more to receive the thanks of all these poor people for all we are doing to stop the Serbs throwing them out of their homes.

It has really been humbling to walk through the huge crowds of people, cheering and calling out "Tony, Tony," as I pass among them, distributing all the clothes left over from our last parish jumble sale.

I shall never forget the tears in the eyes of one old lady who had lost everything, when I presented her with a nearly new electric toaster as a symbol of St Albion's commitment to helping these unfortunate people.

They may not have electricity or bread in these camps, but at least they know that we at St Albion's have not forgotten them.

And, on a very personal note, I have to say that the thousands of people on the hillside calling out my name gave me some idea of what Our Lord must have felt on that first Palm Sunday all those millions of years ago, when he was welcomed as the Saviour of the world.

Of course, I'm not suggesting any parallel! Only pointing out that people out here are pretty grateful for what I am trying to do, in stark contrast, to be honest, to those people back home who seem to spend all their time whingeing and pretending they know more about what is going on than those of us who have rolled up our sleeves and got stuck in.

I expect my friend in Tesco has been very disappointed not to see me at the checkout, so that he can ask me one of his usual silly questions such as "Will it be all over by Christmas then, Vicar?"

Of course, it won't be all over by Christmas. No one ever said it would be, except possibly Mr Campbell, who was no doubt misquoted!

As it says in the words of that wonderful old hymn, "Keep right on to the end of the road, keep right on to the end."

And if that means I've got to come out here to Macedonia to have my picture taken every week until the year 2000, so be it.

And talking of the year 2000, I was telling my new Albanian

friends about our wonderful Millennium Tent.

And, you know, they were so excited that they asked if they could have it to live in.

That's the difference between them and some of the less grateful members of the parish!

Yours (in the footsteps of St Paul in Macedonia!),

Tony

The Vicar's Postbag...

I would like to share with you all a very moving letter I have received from a local doctor and former member of the parish.

Dear Tony,

I have long been an admirer of everything that you are doing at St Albion's. As you know, I had a disagreement with one of your predecessors, Canon Gummidge, as a result of which I left the church and set up my own church, which later merged with the United Liberal Reform Church, which then became the United Liberal and Social Democratic Reform Church. But how I would like to rejoin your Church, provided I could be given an important job to do in keeping with my abilities and status. Please find my CV enclosed.

Yours faithfully,
Dr David Owen.

P.S. I'm afraid I cannot supply the names of any referees as I have fallen out with everyone I have ever met. But I hope this will not count against me!

Obviously, it is a pleasure to welcome home any prodigal son but, as Mr Campbell has explained to Dr Owen, we have not got any parish post suitable for him at the moment, but we will keep his name on file, should any such vacancy arise, which it will not.

OUR THANKS TO...

All who turned out to support **Cherie** and **Mrs Clintstone** (wife of our good friend the Rev. William Jefferson Clintstone, minister of the Church of the Seven Day Fornicators) at their wonderful coffee morning to launch our new parish Childline. As Hillary put it so well, "You know, kids matter! They are the future!"

Mr Sainsbury for the delicious Barbecued GM Vegetarian Soyaburgers at the Parish Bar-B-Q Evening. As Church Warden Mr Cunningham put it: "These things are so safe and so delicious I'm almost tempted to eat one myself!"

TEXT OF THE WEEK

"Take up your bed and work!"

Our Lord's message to the disabled! T.B.

A First For St Albion's!

We have appointed a new "Parish Poet", Mr Motion, who will be writing regular poems in this newsletter on a wide range of important issues. Here is his first effort, which I am sure will be enjoyed by parishioners of all ages, genders and orientations!

MEETING THE VICAR

We met at the pub. And sat
Outside, because it was sunny.
Tony, the vicar, had half a lager and
A bag of
Ready salted crisps.
I had a ploughman's and
A tonic water.
To begin with, conversation was a bit
Stilted.
A No.94 bus went past, like
A great red bus.
Then another. And another.
"Isn't it strange," I observed,
"How the buses come in threes?"
He laughed and it broke
The ice.
After that we got on like
A house on fire.
Or a fire raging through
A house.
"Could I be the parish poet?"
I asked, as we stood in the car park,
Like two men standing in a car park.
He laughed. "We'll be in touch,"
He said.
And he is "in touch", Tony.
What a great
Bloke.

Andrew Motion — *The People's Parish Poet.*

ST ALBION PARISH NEWS

11th June 1999

Hullo!

Some of you will be pleased to hear that I'm not going to be writing about the war this week!

Firstly, because I think I have said all that needs to be said on that subject. And, secondly, because I don't want to say "I told you so", just because peace has broken out. (And it *is* peace, even if it still looks like war at the moment. Sometimes they are quite difficult to tell apart!)

Nothing is gained from rubbing people's noses in it, particularly not our friend in Tesco's, who must be feeling pretty silly now that he has been proved to be so wrong on all his points!

Next time I see him by the checkout counter perhaps he will be good enough to offer an unreserved apology for daring to question someone who knows a lot more than he does about this particular issue (and indeed a good many others!).

Not that I have anything against the healthy expression of contrary views in the parish.

I've always made it clear that I welcome everyone having the chance to have their say.

For example, last week Mr Booth, an out-of-work actor who claims to be Cherie's father, saw fit to hold forth in the Britannia Arms at some length, accusing me of watering down our traditional beliefs and doctrines just to curry popularity.

It is tempting to make a cheap riposte and say that possibly Mr Booth should "water down" the contents of his glass before sounding off in public! But I will resist that temptation, because nothing is gained by indulging in petty name-calling with a pathetic victim of alcohol abuse who is clearly in need of professional help.

Another example concerns someone who plays a rather more elevated role in parish life, namely the Honorary Life President-Elect of the St Albion's Flower Festival (ie, Prince Charles).

At our recent AGM the Prince made a long-winded and, with respect, ill-informed and self-important speech in which he condemned the use of genetically modified flowers in the church, and claimed to have found a number of dead moths and beetles in the chancel, allegedly the victims of what he called "the killer GM lilies" which decorated the altar over the recent Festival of Bank Holiday.

Of course, I welcome the Prince's comments as a valuable contribution to the debate on this issue. But may I just say, again with the greatest possible respect, that in future he would be better advised to keep his mouth shut on matters he knows nothing about. Otherwise he could well find that he never succeeds to his mother's job, which is a purely honorary post anyway and certainly does not entitle him to criticise the views of the properly constituted parish authorities, ie the vicar.

On a happier note, I think we can all be justifiably proud of the recent achievements of the Manchester United football team.

Theirs was a superb team effort, showing what you can achieve when you are united behind a strong leader with a vision.

Well done, Alex Ferguson, who I'm very much hoping will be coming to open the St Albion's Summer Fête this year, even though he has refused.

Yours in victory*,

Tony

*2-1 over Milosevic in injury time!

Notices

■ I am delighted to be able to announce that the St Albion's Grammar School is to be closed down.

As you know, I have always been a great admirer of comprehensive schools, and Cherie and I would have loved our own children to go to one. Sadly, though, these schools aren't any good, which is why we had to send all our children to Our Lady Of The League Tables in the nextdoor parish.

I myself never had the benefit of a comprehensive education, and I had to make do with a private school in Scotland. Still, I haven't done too badly! Which just shows that you can overcome all kinds of handicaps in this life! Honestly! "Education, education, education" — sometimes I think it's all people go on about! T.B.

✝ To Remember In Your Prayers

● Mr Mortimer, one of our older parishioners, who is having another crisis of faith and has recently expressed doubts about the way that the modern St Albion's is moving forward in a vibrant and pivotal way.

Let us pray for John at a time when his brain has clearly become fuddled by advancing age, and perhaps a little too much of that champagne which he is so fond of! T.B

PARISH POSTBAG

Dear Reverend,

I know you're getting a lot of stick these days from everyone else, but I'd just like to say that I think you are fantastic! My lovely tea with you and Cherie in the vicarage was a real highlight of my life, and the bird I brought with me (wasn't she a corker, eh?) had a great time as well.

No wonder you're so popular, vicar, you're a real gent.

Your Number One Fan,
Michael Winner,
3, Death Wish Crescent.

The editor reserves the right to print adulatory letters without cutting a single word. AC

Here's a picture of a Winner! The one on the left! A.C.

ST ALBION PARISH NEWS

25th June 1999

Hullo!

Thank you for all your messages of congratulations on our historic victory in Europe! I hope in due course to be able to thank each one of you personally for supporting the firm line I took over Kosovo.

I must emphasise, of course, that this was not just a vindication of everything I have been saying all along. No, this was a triumph for peace and humanity, and I am very proud to have been the one who recognised this, when a lot of other people seemed to lack the appropriate faith!

I am reminded of the words of the New Testament, "There is more rejoicing in heaven over the one just man than over ninety-nine who get it completely wrong" *(Parable of the Sheep and the Gloats)*.

The last thing I want to do is to make a big song and dance over this victory. So I have decided to hold a low-key two-hour long Service of Thanksgiving, with singing and dancing, with street parties throughout the parish, followed by bonfires.

There will be a half-day holiday for all St Albion's schools, and we shall also have special day-long pealing of the church bells, organised by members of the St Albion's Campanology Society led by Mr Smith and his partner.

Apart from these few informal events, it would be inappropriate to go over the top in marking this wonderful victory for the forces of good over evil, but I hope you will all join me at the fireworks' display which we are holding on the recreation ground.

NB. The PCC will accept no responsibility for any "collateral damage" caused to persons or property by any fireworks which go astray.

Is it surprising, in view of the part I had to play in this great drama on the world stage, that I have inevitably had not as much time as I would have liked for more trivial matters, such as the recent PCC elections for our oecumenical European liaison sub-committee.

The fact that almost no one in the parish bothered to vote is surely a sign that the vast majority of parishioners are so happy with the way we are running the parish that they preferred to enjoy the summer sunshine (not that we've had much of it!) or watch the very entertaining cricket competition which has been showing on the television.

It would be obviously inappropriate to devote any space in the Parish News to the behaviour of a member of the St Albion's Sixth Form Debating Soceity, but we must all have been shocked by the recent antics of young Master William Hague.

To describe him as "smug", "cocky" and "far too pleased with himself" would be unfair, though true. And he may well regret that, in trying to win cheap, short-term popularity with the old people of the parish, he has said so many silly things.

I am certainly not going to descend to his level of personal abuse, but I can only suggest that he would command more respect if he bought himself a good wig!

Yours in triumph!

Tony

A tough moment for the vicar as two of the pupils from St Albion Primary School grill him on the big issues. "What is your favourite colour?" they asked. Tony told Shaznee (left) and Posh (middle) that he liked purple best. And green. And yellow. And red. And orange. And blue. And white. "I like them all".

Notices

■ The Millennium Tent is absolutely on schedule and, thanks to generous recent sponsorship from the local business community, we have been able to complete the previously designated "Religion Zone". This will now focus on the important spiritual values common to everyone in St Albion's and will be renamed "The Money Zone".

■ The Vicar will *personally* be coaching the St Albion's Boys Cricket First XI on the green. He is very worried about declining standards in sports and wants all the boys to get in as much practise as possible — before the green is sold to his friend Mr Walmart for one of his exciting new supermarkets.

Parish Postbag...

Dear Vicar,

Since I was forced to resign as Churchwarden due to circumstances beyond my control, it is quite clear that the running of the parish has been an unmitigated disaster.

While I am second to none in my admiration for my successor Mr Cunningham, I am sure everyone now recognises that he is utterly useless, as is Mrs Beckett and everyone else who has been trying to do my old job. Surely it is time for a concerted campaign to call for the reinstatement of the only person in the parish who knows how to run things properly. Modesty forbids that I should name that person, but I am sure your readers will have no difficulty in identifying the man I have in mind!

Yours faithfully,
P. Mandelson
(Ex-Churchwarden 1997-1999)
Address Withheld.

The Editor reserves the right to print in full all letters written at the suggestion of the Vicar. A. Campbell, Ed.

Parish Discussion Groups

Wednesday.
Mr Darling will give us a short talk on the need for a compassionate answer to the tragic problem of our teenage mothers – *"Lock Up The Lazy Slappers And Withdraw Their Benefits: Is it the only language they understand?"*

Friday.
Mr Straw on *"Does Marriage Have Any Place In The Swinging St Albion's Of Today?"* Do come along and bring your same-sex partner or "significant other". Or just come on your own – there's nothing wrong with single people! T.B.

👍 Thanks to...

Mrs Beckett for the wonderful job she did in organising the recent PCC elections. She has earned herself a good long rest after all her hard work, and will enjoy her early retirement. Perhaps she can spend it on holiday in her caravan, as she did during the most important week in the run-up to the elections.

Thanks a bundle, Margaret! T.B.

HYMNS MODERN AND MODERN
(Additional Anthems and Choruses for Parish Use)

NO. 99 MILLENNIUM HYMN

The day will soon be coming
It's only months away
It all starts on the 1st of January
Hooray! Hooray! Hooray!

(Chorus)

Millennium, Millennium,
It means a thousand years
Millennium, Millennium
Let's all give three cheers

We are with you, Tony
So take us by the hand,
And lead us, heavenly Tony
Into the Promised Land

(Chorus)

Millennium, Millennium,
It means two thousand years
Millennium, Millennium
Let's give two thousand cheers!

(Words C. Falconer)

NO. 101 CHORUS FOR SUNDAY SCHOOLS

I love T-O-N-Y
I love T-O-N-Y
I know I do, I'm sure I do
I love T-O-N-Y
(REPEAT AGAIN)

(Words P. Mandelson)

NO. 100 HYMN FOR USE BY THE TEMPORARILY UNEMPLOYED

We have been given a New Deal
We have been given a New Feel
The deal is real, and feel is real,
And the New Deal is really real!

Stand stand stand on your own two feet
Stand stand stand on your own two feet
Stand stand stand on your own two feet
Nowadays we must compete!

(Words S. Byers)

NO. 96 FOR USE ON ANNIVERSARIES OF VERY IMPORTANT DATES

(e.g. Two years of a vicar's incumbancy)

Happy third way to us
Happy third way to us
Happy third way to St Albion's
Happy third way to us
(bis)

(Words A. Campbell)

NO. 98 FOR HARVEST FESTIVAL

All things bright and beautiful
All creatures great and small
All things wise and wonderful
Monsanto made them all

Each soya bean that whistles,
Each little fish that sings,
They gave potatoes fingers,
They gave the turnips wings.

All things bright and beautiful
All creatures great and small
All things wise and wonderful
Monsanto made them all

(Words J. Cunningham and D. Sainsbury)

ST ALBION PARISH NEWS

9th July 1999

Hullo!

And very much *not* goodbye, whatever some of the older parishioners may have been muttering during my unavoidable absence in Ireland!

Let me begin by thanking all of you for all the wonderful letters you have sent me asking to reappoint Mr Mandelson as our churchwarden.

When I wrote asking you to write these letters, I had no idea that there would be such a response!

There was literally a sackful waiting for me on the vicarage doorstep when I returned home from my mission to bring peace to Ireland!

"It's the sack for you then vicar!" said the postman unhelpfully. I had to explain to him that, like our friend in Tesco, he had got the wrong end of the stick!

The letters all stressed that, although everything in the parish was going extremely well, things might go even better if Peter could come back to lend a helping hand!

And, let's face it, although Peter made clear time and again that he had done nothing wrong, he has now surely more than made amends for whatever it was that he didn't do wrong!

As it says in the Book of Common Blair, "Ye that do earnestly repent of your sins, shall get your jobs back 'ere long" (1999 version).

In fact, Peter has already been doing good work around the Parish, spreading the Gospel (literally, "good news!") about our links with European churches and the necessity of taking the collection in euros.

Peter has done all this off his own bat, with no thought of reward or position, which is why, frankly, it is high time he was given his job back!

He has even been evangelising among the older members of our congregation – the so-called "core parishioners" – who have stopped coming to church ever since he told them they weren't wanted in 1997!

But, goodness me, how we need them to do all those humdrum jobs like knocking on doors, organising the raffles and voting for me in the parish elections!

So, welcome back, Peter – not that you *are* back yet! And well done everybody for getting the message about welcoming the "lost sheep" back into the fold!

As it says in the Bible, "Peter is the rock on which our Church is founded." (Interestingly, the Latin for "rock" is "Mandelson"!)

Yours,

Tony

Valete...

...To **Mr Benn**, who has decided, after 50 years' service to the Parish, to go into the mental asylum, where they have been expecting him for some time. We are all grateful for the huge amount he has achieved in his long and distinguished career, although frankly it is quite difficult to remember any of it! His daughter Hilary, who has taken over his duties, has sent us a contribution that her father made to the *Parish Newsletter* as long ago as 1959, which I am sure you will enjoy!

"How To Make A Good Strong Cup Of Working-Class Tea" by Lord Stansgate (Mr Benn)

1. Take 6 tea-bags and place in an enamel mug (NOT a cup!).
2. Pour on scalding water and leave to infuse for half-an-hour.
3. Prod with pipe stem to ensure maximum flavour.
4. Top up with milk and 16 teaspoons of sugar, to taste.

Perhaps this is the best way to remember him! *T.B.*

Parish Postbag...

Dear Sir,

May I use the columns of the Parish Newsletter to remind parishioners that they are not permitted to drive vehicles on the special "Bus Lane" which has been designated between the Working Men's Club and the church entrance. There has recently been one case where an impatient motorist, who clearly thought he was more important than everyone else, drove out of the traffic jam caused by the bus lane and insisted on driving in his dirty great big "People's Carrier" (reg. no. BLA 1R) right down the section of the carriageway reserved for buses, and made some fatuous excuse about

Yours faithfully,
J. Prescott,
Chair of the Parish,
Integrated Transport
Policy Sub-Committee.

The Editor reserves the right to cut all letters from Mr Prescott on the grounds of space or unintelligibility.

Dr Mowlam writes:

We've chosen for our window, to commemorate a famous Irish saint, St Gerry of Adams. Gerry brought peace to Northern Ireland and it doesn't help to go round suggesting that he brought war to it first.

Let me remind everyone of the story. For many years there was trouble in Ireland and lots of people were blown up. But it doesn't do any good to go around blaming people. The important thing was that Gerry was converted to the ways of peace. he gave up all his weapons, except for the ones he decided to keep.

And ever since then the people of Ireland have lived in harmony, thanks to St Gerry and his Peacemakers.

St. Gerry

Consecration of our new stained-glass window (by local artist
Sir Kenneth Pyne RA) has been postponed until further notice.
We hope it will go off with a bang – probably next May (T.B.)

ST ALBION PARISH NEWS

23rd July 1999

Hullo!

I know there's been a lot of idle gossip around the parish recently suggesting that there has been some kind of a falling-out between myself and that stalwart bastion of the working men's club, John Prescott!

How sad it is that some people seem to have nothing better to do on these lovely long summer days we've been enjoying than to indulge in idle chit chat, manufacturing differences which do not exist!

Let me make it clear once and for all that I am second to none in my admiration for the way John runs the working men's club.

No one could do a better job than John in keeping up morale among the older members of the parish, as he did so effectively last weekend when he opened the car boot sale in aid of the Millennium Tent at the municipal sewage farm!

John may not have had the benefit of a good education like some of us. He may be lacking in some of the social airs and graces.

He may, on occasion, put his foot in it. But that's John, a rough diamond doing a difficult job, and it's not for the rest of us to be judgmental about his failings just because he has more of them than most of us!

And, above all, I have to take issue with this silly idea that I myself am out of touch with the older parishioners and the kind of people who go to John's club.

So let's stop all this silly tittle-tattle and get back to discussing the really important issues that are of concern to us all.

As the Good Book puts it, "Set your sights on the moral ground; for that way lies the victory"(New Labour Bible, Letter from Peter to the Milbankians).

That is why by far the most important moral issue confronting the world today is the barbarous and cruel practice of fox-hunting.

Every civilised man, woman and child is rightly outraged by the sight of these members of the hereditary peerage who take pleasure in regularly dressing-up simply to enjoy inflicting maximum suffering on a poor innocent animal.

From now on, I shall not rest until every vestige of this unspeakable so-called sport is swept away, and everyone who indulges in it is put behind bars!

I was able to make this point very strongly to our friend in Tesco, who once again buttonholed me last week while I was standing in the "Baskets Only" queue.

"What do you know about fox hunting, Vicar?" he said.

"Don't you realise that thousands of jobs depend on it, not to mention all the poor dogs which they will have to put down. You only do it to get a bit of cheap popularity because you've got no idea what to do about Northern Ireland."

At this point, he unfortunately fell backwards into a tasting display of Tesco's own new prawn-flavoured crème fraîche presided over by a lady called Elaine in a fetching straw hat and white coat!

Yours,

Tony

From Mr Campbell, Editor

From now on there will be no more discussion about the vicar's choice of school for his children. This is a private matter and if he chooses to send them to Our Lady of the League Tables rather than St Albion's Sink School that is entirely his own affair. Everyone please note. A.C.

Verses From A Local Poet

When I am Mayor of London
All bus-fares will be free.
I love those London buses
Because they're red, like me!

Ken Livingstone, Proprietor of
The Aquatic Pet Centre,
Newts R Us, The High Street.

Notices

■ As usual, I'm taking my usual break and I shall leave the parish in the capable hands of Mr Prescott. If you have any problems, ring me directly on my mobile 0730-446321 or leave a message with Luigi at the Palazzo Magnifico di Popoli, San Pietro di Mandelsoni.

Parish B-B-Q! News Update!
■ I am thrilled to tell you that at the summer B-B-Q Nick Brown will be putting beef back on the griddle! So now the Summer Menu reads: Chicken Burgers, Tuna Burgers and Veggie Burgers! Well done, Nick and his team. So, no more beefing about this one!! (T.B.)

Parish Postbag...

Dear Everyone,

I keep on hearing that the vicar intends to dispense with my services in his annual rationalisation of the team ministry. It is really shameful that someone like myself, who has given years of faithful service to Tony and the team, can suddenly be

Yours sincerely,
Mrs M. Beckett, Caravan 47B,
Somewhere in France.

All letters from parish office-holders about to be sacked may be shortened for reasons of space. A. Campbell, Editor.

Dear Sir,
I would like to protest
Yours sincerely,
Miss G. Jackson, Dunactin,
Hampstead Way.

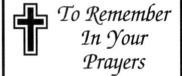

✝ To Remember In Your Prayers

Mr Trimble, at the Northern Irish Mission, who has once again messed everything up by refusing to agree to my quite reasonable suggestions which have been worked out with enormous effort over long days and nights by myself – goodness me, how I've tried – so let's all pray that God knocks some sense into his stupid head. Amen.

ST ALBION PARISH NEWS

6th August 1999

Hullo!

And a very sunny hullo it is too!

I'm not going to claim credit for all the wonderful weather we've been having, obviously! But it is one of the things I promised to sort out when I took over at St Albion's, and it's good to know that we've met our target of a 30 percent improvement in sunny days over the last year!

Some of you will have read this in our parish "end-of-term report", which is now available in Tesco's in the High Street for the very modest sum of £5.99.

Perhaps our friend in Tesco would like to economise on his purchases of South African Chardonnay and buy a copy, so that he can be better informed when he next accosts me in the "8 Items Or Less" queue to make some pathetic point about hospital waiting lists going up!

And let me say that this "Letter To The Tesconians", as I call it, is a fully independent report on all our achievements, not written by me but by a completely unbiassed observer, ie Mr Campbell.

For those of us who are too mean to pay the £5.99 (Mr Benn or Mr Hattersley might know who I am thinking of here!), let me summarise the contents.

And to make it simpler I have listed all the promises I made when I came to the parish, and then shown how I have managed to keep every one of them! ("By their deeds shall ye know them," *Book of Common Blair.*)

1. New-look flower roster	*(done)*
2. New carpet to be ordered for vestry	*(done)*
3. Millennium Window	*(commissioned)*
4. Peace in Northern Ireland	*(on the way!)*
5. An end to world poverty by 2010	*(done)*

And with a record like this, it's hardly suprising that I've decided to keep on with the same team ministry that has come up with such good results!

Look, Our Lord didn't reshuffle the disciples every ten minutes, did he — promoting some and demoting others? He kept the same winning team year in and year out, and that's my policy too!

I don't know who started all those rumours that I was about to sack Mrs Beckett, just because she kept going on holiday in her caravan instead of attending to parish business, but they must feel pretty silly now!

Ditto all those people who were convinced that I was going to replace Mr Cunningham as Church Warden, Mrs Mowlam as head of the Mission to St Gerry's and Mr Prescott for messing up the car parking outside the church!

How ridiculous! As the Good Book has it, "If it ain't broke, don't fix it" *(Book of Proverbs, Ch. 6)*.

And, talking of "breaks", Cherie and I and the family are off for a well-earned one to our favourite haunt in Tuscany, the Castello di Freebi near Siena.

We all hope to recharge our batteries in the olive groves far away from the cares and pressures of parish life!

Not that I am in any way tired or in need of a holiday! But Cherie and the children really do deserve a bit more quality time with me!

There's a lesson there, I feel, for all of us men, isn't there?

Ciao,
Antonio!

The Vicar on Holiday

"Which way, Dad?"
"The Third Way, of course"

Valete...

Mrs Jackson and **Mr Banks**, who are stepping down from the PCC to spend more time auditioning for the role of the Lord Mayor of London in the St Albion's Christmas panto. Good luck to them both, and may the best man win! (Not Mr Livingstone!) T.B.

MARRIAGE BANNS

I would like to publish the banns of marriage between Gordon Brown, bachelor of this parish, and Sarah Macaulay, spinster of the PR-ish of Hobsbawm. This is for the 49th time of asking. If anyone knows of any reason why these two aren't getting married, I'd like to know. T.B.

Parish Postbag

Dear Sir,

I was deeply shocked to hear the Vicar suddenly announcing in the middle of his sermon the other day that he thought fox-hunting was a sin. Some of us thought he must have been at the Communion wine. Otherwise, why did he

Yours sincerely,

Anne Mallalieu, Tally Ho!

Mortimer St John, Sabs.

The Editor reserves the right to cut all letters in favour of fox-hunting for reasons of space. A.C.

My Prayer for Kosovo – as delivered

by myself last week when I was actually there (unlike some of my critics).

Let us pray that all the people may lay aside their age-old hatreds and live together henceforth in peace, harmony and brotherly love. Hey! Forgive and forget, guys! Amen

All parishoners are urged to use this form of address in their private devotions. T.B.

Notices

■ Congratulations to the ladies of the parish who have featured so prominently on my new list of rotas. It just goes to show that women are just as capable as men of doing key parish jobs — like arranging the flowers and organising the teas — and, lets face it, they brighten the place up a bit!

■ Special congratulations to Kate Whoshe who from now on will be in charge of the half-time oranges for St Albion's Soccer XI. Well done, Kate, and good luck.

■ Friday is the feast of the Transfiguration when one leader's followers realised that he was not just some common mortal. Think about it. T.B.

Parish Scrapbook

"He's got the whole world in his hand" *(Letter to the Kosovans, 4. 16)*

Stand by your man! Mrs William Jefferson Clinton takes the vicar's good advice!

Tony shows some old fashioned churchmen what a *modern* vicar wears!

ST ALBION PARISH NEWS

20th August 1999

Hullo!

You may be wondering why my picture is at the top of this newsletter.

The Vicar has gone on holiday and has asked me to take charge of parish business while he is away, enjoying a well-earned rest after all the wonderful work he has been doing for us all.

A lot of my mates in the Working Men's Club have been asking "Hey, John, surely the Vicar is well enough off to pay for his own holidays. And his missus goes out to work as well, working up West in that legal firm, so she must have a few bob in the bank in her own right.

"So, why are they poncing off to some flash palazzo in Italy, at the expense of the Italian taxpayers?"

Let me make it clear, these were not my words. They are just what everyone else in the parish has been saying.

And although I don't necessarily agree with them, I respect their right to have their own opinions.

But I do think that a number of points should be made clear, just so that there is no misunderstanding.

For example, when the Italian police declared five miles of beach out of bounds to the public, so that Tony and his family could enjoy a little well-earned privacy, I am assured that this was not in any way Tony's idea, and that as soon as he realised that it was going to get him bad publicity, he stepped in at once and made it clear that in no way did he want to be given special treatment.

Similarly, you may have heard that the Vicar and his family were permitted to climb up the Leaning Tower of Pisa, something no one else is ever allowed to do, not even the Pope!

Well, all I can say is what a tribute to our Vicar that he is seen as someone so special, as opposed to all the thousands of ordinary, decent working-class people who go away disappointed.

Anyway, enough of all this carping about the Vicar's holiday arrangements, understandable though it is.

I think we all wish Tony and Cherie a good rest, and my message to them both, as I put through on the mobile, is that, since they went away, everything back here in the parish has been running as smoothly as they could want.

So, as far as I am concerned, they should feel free to stay away as long as they like, and good riddance!

And, while I'm about it, there's another point I'd like to make, which is about the part played in parish business by Mr Campbell (no offence to our Editor, who is also, I am glad to say, on holiday!).

Nowadays, it seems to be the fashion for everyone of any importance to employ the services of "advisors" and so-called "spin-doctors" who go around spreading rumours and lies about decent folk trying to do their job to the best of my ability.

I do not think it is any of Mr Campbell's business whether I use hair dye or not, just because I am getting a bit grey around the temples, or when I occasionally use words in the wrong complex, just because they've all been to posh schools.

In my view there are too many pansies hanging around the back of the vicarage for my liking. No names, but all I can say is that if I was in charge, I wouldn't touch that Mr Mandelson with a barge pole.

Yours in Christian fellowship!

John Prescott, *pp. The Vicar.*

SUGGESTION BOX

Acting-Editor JP writes: "Some people have suggested that this parish newsletter could do with a bit of livening up. Amen to that! You should see some of the rubbish that gets sent in by would-be contributors, such as the poem we had last week on the Eclipse from Mrs Jay, the manager of our old folk's home.

The Eclipse

For a brief moment, the world
                    went dark,
Not a bird sang nor a dog did bark.
But then the sun came out once
                    more
When Tony returned to his native
                    shore!

Can't we do better than that, comrades? How about a nice poem about the Working Men's Club?

A Warm Welcome To...

The Rev. Kennedy, who is to succeed our old friend
Mr Ashdown as Minister in Charge of the United Liberal
Democratic Reform Church.

JP writes: Congratulations to young Charles Kennedy, whom I am
sure will do a good job, even though, not to mince words, he is only
a small fish in a small pond. There has been a lot of talk about our
two churches working more closely together, which is all very well,
but if you want my frank opinion, we at St Albion's can get on quite
well enough without them. Good luck, Charlie!

Postcard From The Vicar

Dear John,

*As you can see, we are
here in Pisa for the day
(That's not Mushy Pisa as
you have down at the
Working Men's Club!).*

*And look! As you can see,
the famous tower is not
leaning to the right or to the
left. It is pointing straight up
(the Third Way!).*

*I hope you will under-
stand the significance of
this.*

Tony

The Acting Editor regrets that it
has not been possible to
reprint the Vicar's entire
postcard for reasons of space.

RESPONSES FOR EVENSONG

Just a reminder that this week we'll be introducing a new, modern and relevant set of responses into the service.

So here they are for everyone to "familiarise" themselves, so we can all join in properly!

VICAR:
> **Let us remember in our prayers all those members of the parish who work so selflessly for the good of the whole community. By whom I mean, of course, our local businessmen. As Our Lord himself said, "Blessed are the wealth creators; for they shall be rewarded on earth."**

VICAR:
> **Who wanteth to be a millionaire?**

CONGREGATION:
> **We all do.**

VICAR:
> **Is that your final answer?**

CONGREGATION:
> **Yes, indeed it is.**

VICAR:
> **Do you want to ask a friend?**

CONGREGATION:
> **We doeth not.**

VICAR:
> **Correct.**

That is the spirit we need! T.B.

ST ALBION PARISH NEWS

3rd September 1999

Hello,

It always takes a bit of adjustment when you come back from your holidays, doesn't it? It's hard to get back into the routine when you've been having a nice time in the sunshine and you have to come back to the rainy weather and the same old problems that haven't gone away – or may even have got worse if the person you left in charge wasn't up to it.

And it doesn't help when people begrudge you even your hard-earned holiday.

"Why can't the vicar go to Butlins at Skegness?" asks one parishioner. "Why can't he pay for his own holiday like the rest of us?" asks another.

Honestly! You only have to look at the Good Book to see how Our Lord himself gladly accepted the hospitality of rich supporters. Even his tomb itself was provided by a wealthy businessman.
Look! All your vicar was doing was being polite in taking up a few modest offers from well-wishers in Italy and France. Remember the words of the Gospel, "In my friend's house there are many rooms and they are yours for the summer." *(The Cook of St Thomas 7.13)*

And as for those of you who complained about Cherie and me going to watch the famous horse-race in Siena on the grounds that it is cruel – well, what can I say?

It would look pretty churlish to criticise the age-old customs and traditions of your host country. Just imagine if I invited my Italian counterpart to go to a fox-hunt and he refused on the grounds that it was cruel?

Imagine how well that would go down?

And, anyway, it was a marvellous spectacle to see the red team come in way ahead of the useless blue team under their leader Williama di Tori whose horse gave way under him on the first corner, much to the delight of the onlookers!

So, the moral is surely "When in Rome, do as the Romans do." *(Romans, 7.18)*

Now, closer to home. I was extremely saddened to find that in my absence the Poor Box in the church had been broken into and the lead taken from the roof. It is not for me to point the finger of suspicion, but it is surely no coincidence that a party of gypsies have recently camped on the wasteland on the other side of the cemetery.

Mr Straw from the Neighbourhood Watch said it was bound to be them, as it always was. I told him that this was not exactly a Christian sentiment but was one with which, nevertheless, it was hard to disagree.

It is not for me to tell parishioners what to do, but it is surely time to band together and persuade the gypsies to move on somewhere else.

Yours, Tony

 ## Parish Postbag...

Dear Sir,

As a long-standing and vewy important pawishioner may I congwatulate the Vicar on his choice of an agweeable holiday destination in Tuscany. What would people think of the Vicar and his delightful wife, Chewie, were they to go to some dweadful bed and bweakfast in Wamsgate full of working class wiff-waff? Surely it would weflect badly on the whole pawish?

>   *Yours sincerely,*
>   *Mr Woy Jenkins.*
>   *St Twopez.*

This letter was transcribed from my answering machine by my secretary. It has been included in its entirety, as are all letters defending the vicar.
Alastair Campbell, Editor.

WARNING

Could the younger members of the parish please leave Mr Monsanto's allotment ALONE!! He is experimenting with some new seeds which could be of great benefit to rich people throughout the world. So keep off! Okay?! T.B.

✝ To Remember In Your Prayers

Poor Miss Widdecombe, a single lady who lives alone with her old mother and who has been making a nuisance of herself in the parish, accosting Mr Straw and others in the course of their work, shouting obscenities and talking nonsense loudly to herself.

She has even written a poison pen letter to the vicarage accusing the Vicar of "scrounging off foreigners". Obviously, I have forgiven her (and merely reported her to the police), but I can see that it must be very annoying for everyone else.

So we pray that this poor, distressed lady, who has sadly not been blessed with good looks, may find some useful occupation for her undoubted energy. Perhaps she might stay at home and receive counselling over the internet. T.B.

Mrs Jay, Matron of the St Albion's Home for Distressed Gentlefolk, writes:

*P*lans for the new-look Home are moving along apace, I am pleased to report. Long-term residents have been asked to complete the following sentence in not more than 75 words: "I think I should be allowed to stay on at the home because..."

This will soon sort out the deserving from the undeserving, some of whom are so far gone they cannot remember their own names, let alone write them.

Hint: Only three words are actually needed to complete the sentence: "I love Tony".

Mrs Jay (Daughter of the Reverend Callaghan).

ST ALBION'S TEA TOWEL

A charming picture of the Team Ministry
created by the pupils of St Albion's Primary School

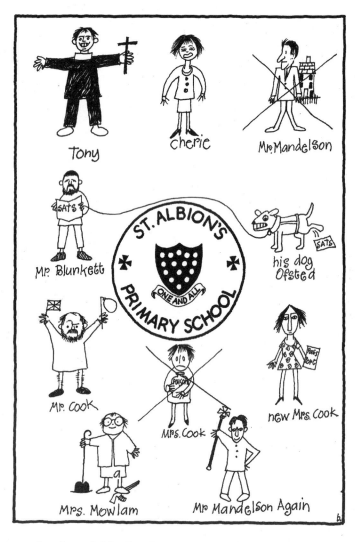

**Copies of this Tea Towel are available from the
Church Coffee Shop (price £32.99).**

The Ideal Christmas Present